AF291456

The Bard
of Colour,
Robert Rose

Dedicated to all those who have suffered discrimination and disrespect on account of diversity or disability

The Bard of Colour, Robert Rose

THE LIFE OF A POET AND ACTIVIST IN THE NINETEENTH CENTURY

GLYNIS COOPER

PEN & SWORD HISTORY

AN IMPRINT OF PEN & SWORD BOOKS LTD.
YORKSHIRE – PHILADELPHIA

First published in Great Britain in 2026 by
PEN AND SWORD HISTORY
An imprint of
Pen & Sword Books Ltd
Yorkshire – Philadelphia

ISBN 978 1 03611 032 1

Typeset in Times New Roman 12/16
by SJmagic DESIGN SERVICES, India.
Printed and bound in the UK by CPI Group (UK) Ltd.

The Publisher's authorised representative in the EU for product safety is
Authorised Rep Compliance Ltd., Ground Floor, 71 Lower Baggot Street,
Dublin D02 P593, Ireland.
www.arccompliance.com

For a complete list of Pen & Sword titles please contact
PEN & SWORD BOOKS LIMITED
George House, Units 12 & 13, Beevor Street, Off Pontefract Road, Barnsley,
South Yorkshire, S71 1HN, England
E-mail: enquiries@pen-and-sword.co.uk
Website: www.pen-and-sword.co.uk

or

PEN AND SWORD BOOKS
1950 Lawrence Rd, Havertown, PA 19083, USA
E-mail: uspen-and-sword@casematepublishers.com
Website: www.penandswordbooks.com

Contents

Acknowledgements

First and foremost acknowledgement is due to Professor Michael Wood who gave me the idea for writing this book.

Secondly acknowledgement is due to John McGuirk, Director of University Library Services, St George's University, Grenada. He loved the Caribbean and its people and he encouraged me in the writing of this book.

Grateful acknowledgments are also due to the staff at Pen & Sword for their patience, understanding, and hard work in editing and publishing my work; and also to my family and friends for encouragement and support.

Introduction

I sadly stand alone too oft to sigh
When pondering on that land so far away;
Alas! No kin are near me should I die,
There's none to soothe me in life's waning day.

A wanderer here, oh! for me who would mourn
If the vast sea of life should o'er me close?
Home of my childhood! May I safe return
To thee, then smiling sink to my repose!

The words of a long-forgotten poet lamenting his absence from his home, an unnamed land far from England, and the family he left behind him. The 19 June 2024 marked an anniversary few knew about, but it was a significant date in the cultural history of Manchester, marking the 175th anniversary of the death of the poet who wrote those words of longing. He was a well-educated man of private means who wrote competent, sometimes reasonably good, poetry, although with a tendency to be mournful and verbose, and he spent around three quarters of his life in Liverpool and Manchester, destined never to return to 'that land so far away'. Quite a different fate awaited him, but what earned him a place in the history books is that he was black, and he was Manchester's first black poet.

Now, 175 years after his death, with the advent of the internet and digitised records, it should have been possible to put flesh on the bones of this enigmatic man. A little under 200 years is not a huge span of time, but less is known about Robert Rose than poets who died, hundreds, or even thousands, of years ago. Homer, the Greek poet and historian, author of the *Iliad* and the *Odyssey* in the eighth century BC; Virgil, a Roman poet who wrote several major works, including the *Aeneid*, in the first century BC; Li Bai and Du Fu, two prolific Chinese poets of the eighth century; and Geoffrey Chaucer who wrote *The Canterbury Tales* in the fifteenth century; are all better known and better documented than Robert Rose, a mid-nineteenth century poet who played an important part in the emerging Manchester literary scene, and who held the unique position of being Manchester's first black poet. Some questions may never be answered, but some insight into the essence of this man, his character, his problems, the passionate beliefs he held and the prejudice he faced, brings Robert Rose out from the murky historical gloom to which he has been consigned and restores him to his rightful place in the history of poetic literature.

Chapter One

'Home of my childhood, may I safe return to thee...'

When relating information about little known people or incomplete events a favourite phrase of modern newspapers is to begin their report with 'what do we know...? In the case of Robert Rose what we know is painfully minimal:

- He was literate and he knew the Classics
- He had a private income, source unknown
- He lived and worked in Liverpool for a time (address and profession unknown)
- He gave an impassioned speech on abolition and emancipation in Liverpool in 1835
- He wrote poetry from 1835–49, including a poem on the coronation of Queen Victoria
- He moved to Manchester and lived at two verifiable addresses
- He was vice chairman of the famed Sun Inn Poets in 1841
- He was attacked in Brazennose Street, Manchester, in the summer of 1841
- He died of delirium tremens in Salford on 19 June 1849
- He was buried in plot 6087 in Manchester General Cemetery

It is not a great deal on which to build an entire biography and the challenge was, at times, almost overwhelming. Much that seemed promising ended in a blind alley. Chetham's Library hold his notebook, but it only covers the years 1840–5. If he kept other notebooks or diaries they have been lost to history. There is no trace of him in births, marriages, and deaths records, slavery records or immigration records. Liverpool has little information apart from the mention of the dinner at which Rose gave his speech on slavery. His speech was published and reprinted several times but there is no copy of it on public access in England. He never published a volume of his poetry, although he published three poems in pamphlet form and a few were included in contemporary anthologies. However, there was one light at the end of the tunnel of no information about him: Robert Rose liked to see his work in print in local newspapers; mostly, it has to be said, Liverpool newspapers, even long after he had moved to Manchester. A lengthy and detailed trawl through the British Newspaper Archive eventually revealed a hitherto hidden cache of his poetical work, critiques, his letters answering criticisms, and such biographical details as have survived. His story is not complete but at last there is a biography and a collection of work to do some justice to the Bard of Colour, Manchester's first black poet.

The pure naked longing for the homeland to which Robert Rose yearned to return is expressed in an early poem, long before his realisation that he would never return to the land of his birth. The home that he so sadly missed and lamented was, by his own admission, Berbice, in what was formerly British Guiana on the South American continent. It lay along the Berbice River in Guiana and from 1627–1792 it was a colony of the Dutch East India Company. Between 1792 and 1815 it became a Dutch colony before being officially ceded to the British in 1815. Berbice lost its own identity in 1831, when it was merged with Demerara-Essequibo to become British Guiana, until gaining independence as Guyana in 1966. These colonies, together with Suriname, were known to the Dutch as the Wild Coast Colonies and lay between the Orinoco and Amazon rivers. Berbice originally had only three towns: Fort Nassau, New Amsterdam and Rose Hall. The official religion was Calvinism, due to the influence of Scottish Highlanders who owned most of the sugar and cotton plantations. In 1763 there was a massive slave rebellion in Berbice which lasted for over a year, but the main outcome was the large-scale execution of what were seen as errant slaves illegally protesting their imagined grievances. Berbice is a hot and humid area close to the coast where much of life centres around the river, boats and the port of New Amsterdam. Jaguars, sloths, monkeys and otters roam the rainforests and there are plenty of the scarily ubiquitous snakes such as anaconda, boas, vipers, and pythons (the latter said to be a particular problem by J.A. Froude in his book on the *English in the West Indies*, published in 1888). There was also a variety of tropical birds which included horned screamers, great tinamous, toucans, and the hoatzin, which is the national bird of Guyana. A multitude of natural foods grew in the West Indies and the collection of varieties would not disgrace an upmarket delicatessen today. Bananas (which West Indians called figs); thick-skinned fragrant green oranges; sugar cane; sweet 'sop' (a green and purple strawberry as large as an orange); custard apple; grapes; avocados (called alligator pears in Berbice); red peppers; green coconuts tinged with orange; yams; and a variety of pulses of various kinds and hues. It would have been an exotic, colourful, ideal adventure playground for an inquisitive little boy who spent his early childhood roaming freely around the river, discovering the small daily wonders of life, and perhaps dreaming of going to sea when he grew up.

The British Empire had crashed into this tropical paradise in 1796. Berbice, originally founded as a Dutch colony early in the seventeenth century, was taken by the British in 1796 along with the neighbouring colonies of Essequibo and Demerara. However, as mentioned earlier, the colonies were not officially ceded to Britain until 1815, and during the intervening turbulent period few records, if any, were kept. It was during this time that Robert Rose was born to a white father and a mother of colour. The plantations of Berbice and its neighbours at that time were mainly sugar plantations, although some coffee, cotton and cocoa were grown as well, but most of the plantations during this period were owned by Scottish Highland families and worked by African slaves. Some slaves were well treated, but many were badly beaten and abused on a regular basis by their masters, and James Beckford (in his autobiography *Christian Labour in the West Indies...,* London, 1890) wrote: 'What I saw in the days of slavery ... can never be told ... it could not be written ... it is too bad to be put into human phrase and published.'

Fevers were endemic, particularly yellow fever, carried by mosquitos and, ironically, brought to the Caribbean on African slave ships. Short lives and frequent deaths were common. The plantation owners were far from home and often without their families; and so too were the military personnel sent to keep order and protect the plantations. Both Dutch and British white men sought comfort with African slave women, or women of the indigenous population. At one time, it was a custom for the sons of the white men to go out in the afternoons and choose a woman from among the slave workers to amuse them for a few hours. The women had absolutely no say in the matter. Refusal could lead to a savage beating at best. Needless to say there were a considerable number of mixed-race illegitimate births, and the Creoles, as West Indies mixed-race offspring of European and African heritage were known, had their own unique languages and cultures. Nevertheless, among these often enforced relationships there were some genuine love stories, and it is tempting to think that Robert Rose might have been a product of mutual affection rather than casual rape because, although his father remains unknown, he made full provision for his son's emigration, education, business training and future lifestyle.

As far as official records are concerned, Robert Rose seems to have come from nowhere; his life is documented in careful terms which gave absolutely nothing away as to who he was, where he came from, what he did, when or how he arrived in England, or of the Liverpool MP said to have sponsored him with an annual income. Until Robert Rose stood up, after a public dinner in Liverpool one summer's evening in 1835, to give an impassioned speech, on the abolition of slavery and emancipation, no one had heard of him outside of his immediate circle of acquaintances. No one knew him well, and no one seemed to claim him as either family or friend. He was like the man from nowhere; but this man was very different. He was real and genuine and alive, passionate about what he believed, and he was not afraid to say so. He was educated and cultured. He wrote and lectured on poetry, and he penned a celebratory poem for the coronation of Queen Victoria in 1838. He should have been easy to identify. He was of mixed race, and, very unusually for those of mixed race in 1820s–30s Liverpool, he was what was termed a 'gentleman'. Although he worked, he had 'private means'. He dressed well. He spoke well. He spent well. Yet he remains a complete mystery.

There appears to be no British family to whom he belongs. There is no biography of him. There are no images of him. There are painfully few personal details. As a general rule, the more you discover, the less you know about him. The nearest we come to knowing anything much at all is from a journalist called John Evans who wrote for the Mercury group of newspapers; shortly before the death of Robert Rose Evans wrote a couple of pieces about him which appeared in the *Nottingham and Newark Mercury* and the *Stockport Mercury*. His article was mostly about Rose's poetry and his abilities as a poet. It was complimentary in tone and emphasised that the abilities and talents of people of colour were equal to those of any race or creed. He finally summarised Rose's life history in just a couple of paragraphs towards the end. John Evans (*Nottingham Mercury* 1849) believed:

> that Mr Rose was born in Berbice, but in what year we are unable to state; he appears, however, now to be about forty-five years. In early life he left the land of his birth and arrived in England at the neighbouring port of Liverpool. He was sent to school in the suburbs of that town and was, in the course of time, removed to another

academy near London. After a period elapsed, he retraced his steps to the north, and completed his studies at Green Row, on the borders of Scotland. It was at the latter place, probably, that he received many of the poetical impressions he has since manifested. He was here surrounded with all the magnificent scenery of the Scotch [*sic*] mountains on the one hand, and Skiddaw and the loft summits of Cumberland on the other, with the beautiful Solway Firth pursuing its silvery course between. Such an eloquence of nature as he must have encountered here, would be sure to produce its effects upon a mind already predisposed towards partaking of wildness and sublimity in the creation. The seed was sown in good time, and has, for a certainty, come forth abundantly.

The mysteries begin right away. No one seemed to know when he was born. Rose never mentions his date of birth. Did he even know it? He died in June 1849, and, after his post-mortem examination, the coroner was informed that Rose was about 43 years old when he died, so this would give him a date of birth from around 1805–07. Rose knew he was born in Berbice, later British Guiana; but between 1795 and 1815, the British were involved in a lengthy takeover of territories in the West Indies from the Dutch with the result that neither side kept birth, marriage, death, or slavery records for those twenty years. It is therefore quite conceivable that Rose never knew his actual date of birth.

How did Robert Rose get his name? He was born to a dark-skinned mother, of African or West Indian descent, and a white father, very likely Scottish, both of whose identities are unknown. It was customary for slave children to take the surname of the parents' slave master but Rose says he was born 'a free man'. In British Guiana during the years of slavery the status of a child usually followed that of its mother which meant that the mother of Robert Rose was not enslaved to any master, and this might mean she was of West Indian rather than African origin. Rose, on the other hand, believed he was a Creole, which would indicate his mother was of African descent. However, it is quite possible that she had been a slave but was manumitted, either by Robert Rose's father or by someone else. Both the names Robert and Rose are of Scottish origin, and indeed it was mostly Highlanders who held the huge sugar plantations of the West Indies, but there is no Rose plantation holder in or around Berbice at the time Rose was born. However, there was an individual named Robert Rose whose brother, Alexander, was a local surgeon. Alexander died in 1805 and his brother Robert died early in 1806. It is possible that this Robert Rose could have fathered the poet Robert Rose, and died around the time he was born (maybe of one of the endemic fevers which killed so many) but, in that case, who would have subsequently taken him back to England for education, work, training, and supported him financially throughout his life? Rose himself seemed to believe that he had no English family for in that poem on his childhood he writes: 'Alas! No kin are near me should I die…' There is a remote possibility that Robert Rose came from Rose Hall and took his surname from the place but, with his silence on the matter and the complete absence of records, that can only be conjecture.

John Evans had stated that Rose was educated at Green Row Academy (run by Joseph Saul), close to Whitehaven on the banks of the Solway Firth. However, in 1819, the year he was supposedly at the academy, there are no records of him having attended that school; nor in 1818 nor in 1820. Not many of this school's records are still extant (there are none before 1816) but Robert Rose does not feature in any of them. Nevertheless, it is obvious from his writing that he had received a good Classical education. In the first verse of his poem 'Poesy on a Winter's Night' (in his notebook held by Chetham's) he displays some detailed knowledge of Classical writers:

> 'Tis cheerful on some snowy winter night
> When the lone wind is rattling at our door
> A guest we'll not let in by fireside bright
> O'er poesy's inspired page de poso

Then we are happy Homer, Virgil, Pope,
Dante, Ariosto, Tasso, greats
Afford to eager minds' unbound scope
As Milton whose high genius doth make
With his 'Scien-isle' and the vast likening
Of Shakespeare circling the whole earth and sky
And Byron whose works envious men want to blight
Whose tomb in great hearts gives his foes the lie
A host of others, sire 'twere vain to name
Who gaze emblazoned on the rolls of fame.

It is possible he was enrolled under another name, but a more likely explanation would be that if he did attend the Green Row Academy he was tutored apart from the other boys because of his skin colour, so his name was left off the published school registers. Rose was proud of his Classical education. He knew his Classical authors and he liked to boast that he could recite eight of the twenty four books of the *Iliad*. If this is true, it is far more likely that he had time on his hands and learned them somewhere like Green Row rather than at a local village or inner-city school.

Subsequently, according to Evans, after receiving his education, the future poet had returned to Liverpool to work in a commercial house 'training for business' although again there is no information to be found. The census returns before 1831 are not fully detailed and staff records from businesses of the time, if they ever existed, have either not been kept or have not survived. No occupation was given for Rose in the 1841 census either, but that is hardly surprising because he had given up his day job by that time. There have also been two world wars since the lifetime of Robert Rose, and Liverpool, like Manchester and other cities, was heavily damaged in the German Blitz of 1940–2 so many records have been destroyed.

The only member of his family that Robert Rose appears to acknowledge, or even to remember, is his mother. He never mentions siblings or grandparents or any other members of an extended family, which many other slaves in the West Indies do. However, in a couple of his poems there is a mention of sisters, though not his own. One is in the 'Cypress Wreath', which is a lament for the untimely death of a young woman and was written for her family. However, in his sonnet on the 'The Lyre' he mentions sisters as a loving memory. Rose always loved a play on words and, although it is entirely possible he had siblings, sisters of whom he was fond, in Berbice there is a town named Sisters which grew up near a large sugar plantation. Rose simply said he lived in Berbice but he never said where in Berbice.

THE LYRE

> Yes! 'tis a bitter thought! I prithee, go,
> And leave me lonely to my chosen theme;
> Albeit 'tis not of joy, but of deepest woe',
> T'is more than all mirth's mock'ry can redeem.
> Oh! Let me, at this solitary time.
> Recall familiar shapes unto my mind, –
> Still dear, as to the swain the merry chime
> Of bells near his blest home where sisters kind
> Again may thrill him with love's harmony.
> Yet a sad thought will shade his manly brow,
> That those he fondly lov'd in days gone by
> May be where he, and all, alas! must bow:
> Thus to the children of the golden lyre,
> Such phantom-thoughts oft check the glowing fire.

There is no way of knowing the truth but, if he did have sisters of whom he was genuinely fond, it might be expected that, as with his mother, he might surely have tried to sail to the West Indies at least once. Many ships left Whitehaven and Liverpool bound for the West Indies, but Rose does not seem to have ever ascertained his family's whereabouts. If he did, there is no longer any trace of his discoveries.

This also begs the question of why he was taken at such an early age to England for education and work. He was almost certainly illegitimate and would have spent his young formative years (until about the age of 7 at least) with his mother, as was customary. There are, to date, absolutely no records and no clues of how, or when, or with whom, he came to England. A possible explanation may lie in the aforementioned fact that although Berbice came under British rule, it was not actually ceded to Britain by the Dutch until 1815. Technically, therefore, its citizens remained Dutch until that point, which might have presented bureaucratic difficulties in Robert Rose leaving the colony for England until all the formalities were completed. Rose would have been about 9 in 1815 if his birth date of 1806 is correct; but even a year or so either side meant that he was still very much a child in 1815. Another factor might have been fears of a rebellion at this time, similar to the notorious Berbice slave rebellion of 1763, and there would still have been living memory of this episode in 1815. The Dutch mainly grew cotton, coffee and tobacco on inland plantations, but the British favoured sugar plantations in the coastal regions as the demand for sugar was increasing. Sugar plantations were harder work and demanded more slave labour. This caused resentment on the part of slaves and indeed there were rebellions in neighbouring Demerara (whose name has been immortalised as that of the light brown sugar granules often served with coffee) in 1809, 1812 and 1823.

However, the only evidence we really have for how, why and when Rose left Berbice is pure conjecture. Rose's longing for his homeland is expressed in his poem of his childhood with an admission that, as an adult, he does not even know if his mother is still alive:

…well I know the scythe
Of restless time is ever busy here
Perchance, and neath the thought the heart must writhe,
That mother hath departed from this sphere…

Therefore, the break must have been complete, but that unknown mother would never have forgotten him. Today such an action would constitute an act of the utmost cruelty, damaging to both mother and child. His mother may well have been illiterate, but illiterate people have found ways of communication other than writing for centuries. To have her cut out of his life so completely must have been constituted either for a very good reason concerning his welfare, or as an act of appalling and uncaring cruelty. Yet he seems to have made no attempt to contact her. As a young adult he lived and worked in Liverpool and ships regularly sailed from that port for the West Indies. He was a bright, literate individual and, if he could remember his country with such longing, he would surely have had some idea of where he had lived as a young child and how to try to find his mother.

He is equally reticent about his father. Is this because he was sworn to absolute secrecy for reasons unknown and careless mention of his birthplace could have identified his father; or did he simply not know who his father was? England during the early decades of the nineteenth century must have been a great culture shock to a little boy who had left the warm vibrant shores of the Caribbean to spend three weeks or so crossing the Atlantic, a perilous and uncomfortable business in itself, to the drab grey skies, noise and bustle of an industrial English port. Life would have appeared cold and grim at best to a young lad used to more colourful and exotic climes. If he did indeed subsequently attend Green Row Academy on the banks of the Solway Firth he must have shivered in the icy winds of the northern British winter.

Chapter Two

'What are thou doing in the busy town...'

Rose said he came to England as a young child. He would almost certainly have landed either in Liverpool or Whitehaven, both major ports for ships sailing from the West Indies. Around the time that Rose would have first met John Evans in 1840, a gentleman named Edwin Keet – an unknown friend of Rose and about to embark on a journey to Italy – wrote a farewell poem, rather than a letter, to Rose. He began with two Classical quotes in deference to Rose's knowledge of the Classics, before writing his own poetic tribute:

Fear and hope, I deem, are fables all,
And life's whole course but one protracted dream!
Eternal Power! When shall I wake to rest
This wearied brain on truth's immortal breast.
(Maetastasio)

Virgil's humble tenement: a low
Plain wall remains, a little sun-gilt heap,
Grotesque and wild, the gourd and olive fan
Their amorous flies, mingling with the vine
Who drops her purple clusters thro' the green!
Here of the meek, good man, the lofty bard
Framed the celestial song, or social walked
With Horace and the ruler of the world,
Happy Augustus!
(Dyer)

Following the quotes, Keet pens his own poignant farewell to Robert Rose:

Hail, Bard of Colour! With complexion brown.
Bard of sweet music, warbling mid the spheres,
What art thou doing in the busy town
Where losses, gains, divide all hopes and fears?

Who now surrounds thy hospitable board;
Who greets thy recitations with applause;
Who, Daniel like, reposes 'neath thy gourd:
Who from the classic fount pure nectar draws?

In colloquy divine we passed the night,
Urania's sparkling mantle o'er us thrown,
When, through the shutters gleams the morning light,
Our brighter visions too, too soon were flown!

Distance divides us now, but o'er my soul
Past scenes return a solemn, wandering train;
The wheels of life pass onward to their goal,
And we, perchance, may never meet again!

Thou, from hot India's sunny, stormy isles,
A stranger cam'st to Albion's rock-girt shores;
Her hardy sons did greet thee with their smiles
Where Solway's flood oft to the tempest roars.

A mentor! O'er thy genius watchful kind,
Kindled the bright, th' undying mental ray;
A sordid traffic could not bind thy mind
Panting for regions of immortal day!

Still soar sublime above the common walk;
Avoid the noise of the vociferous crowd;

Heed not the envious sneer the slanderer's talk;
Condemn the scoffer, and defy the proud!

Thy friend, who now in sadness pens this lay,
Departing to Italia's far-famed shore,
Hears in the breeze of night some spirit say,
'Bid him addio! Ye shall meet no more!
(Edwin Keet c.1840)

This writer obviously knew Rose well for a time and liked him very much. Keet describes Rose as 'brown' rather than black, although that may be just a case of errant etymology.

He gives brief tantalising insights into moments of Rose's life and he refers to Rose's legendary generous hospitality. Keet also refers to Rose's unknown mentor, but he gives no clues at all as to whom that might have been. More importantly, however, he seems to confirm that Rose arrived in Whitehaven on the Solway Firth close to the Scottish borders:

Thou, from hot India's sunny, stormy isles,
A stranger cam'st to Albion's rock-girt shores;
Her hardy sons did greet thee with their smiles
Where Solway's flood oft to the tempest roars.

Rose therefore may have entered Britain via Whitehaven, a major nineteenth-century port for West Indian trade on the Solway Firth, which makes the claims that he attended the Green Row Academy near Whitehaven much more credible, even though he is not listed in the extant official school registers. Whitehaven, in Cumbria, lies at the entrance to the Solway Firth, some 38 miles south from the Scottish border town of Carlisle. It was, at that time, the fifth largest port in England. Originally a major port for coal shipments and the trans-Atlantic slave trade in the eighteenth century, by

Robert Rose's time it had become one of the main ports for West Indies trade.

John Evans simply states that Rose was 'occupied in a commercial house in Liverpool'. What that might have been is not known. He does not comment on how or why Rose went to Liverpool, where he lived or what he did. Liverpool had grown rich on the triangular transatlantic slave trade and the import of cotton. It had become a financial centre second only to that of London, and in 1715 the first commercial wet dock in the world had been built in the city with capacity for 100 ships. The rapid commercial growth of Liverpool led to a population increase of over 1,300 per cent in the eighteenth century, from 6,000 to 80,000, and the opening of a US Consulate there in 1790. The business area of the city was centred around the town hall (built in Georgian times on the High Street near the cathedral), Exchange Flags Square (behind the town hall), and Castle Street. Initially, many commercial buildings contained offices in the upper storeys over warehousing facilities below, but by Rose's time it was likely that they were all mostly used as offices. Ironically, India Buildings, one of the first office blocks, was built in 1833 during Rose's time in the city. These offices were used to house merchants, marine businesses, banks, insurance companies, lawyers, etc. Given Rose's original intention to return to Berbice and use his experience there, it is probable that he worked either in a merchant's office or for a shipping line, as it is likely that he intended to become involved in some kind of trading which would have been beneficial to his homeland. Rose would doubtless have chosen Liverpool because it was a larger, wealthier and more important port even than Whitehaven, and it lay conveniently close to the heartlands of the north-west industrial millscapes. It was probably warmer as well.

Robert Rose continued to remain coy about where, and with whom, he lived in Liverpool. During the late 1830s his poetry was published extensively in Liverpool newspapers, but there appears to be little trace of him in Liverpool, apart from his attendance and speech at Lord Brougham's dinner in 1835, and a rumour that he was popular with co-workers wherever he was employed because of his private means and his reputation for hospitality. However, the 1841 census shows a Helen Rose living at Mount Pleasant, which lies about two thirds of a mile from the commercial centre of Liverpool. In 1798 Helen (née Binny, b.1774) had married a man named Robert Rose (b.1774 in Scotland), and they had a daughter, Anne, in 1802. This Robert Rose is recorded as having died in 1805 in Demerara (the neighbouring state to Berbice). Was Helen Rose linked to the poet's family or perhaps to his benefactor? The suggestion of any such link is extremely tentative but it is all we have. It is also possible that Rose was born under a different name and only adopted his Scottish name once he had arrived in Britain. The real question is why all the secrecy, if secrecy it was? Since Robert Rose's birth date is only approximate, he could have been born in 1804–5 not 1806, but, if he was the son of Helen Rose's husband, he must have been financially provided for from the moment of his birth. However, in the original copy of the census the profession given for this Robert Rose is that of a dentist. It has always been assumed Rose worked in commerce but there is absolutely no evidence to support this theory except for a reference in the article by John Evans. Is it possible Rose could have intended to help his people in a different way to that of commerce. If he actually was the son of Helen Rose's dead husband then he would have had an uncle, Alexander, who had been a surgeon. However, as with so much of the Robert Rose story, there is absolutely no way of knowing the actual truth, of whether the person with the same name who lived at Mount Pleasant really was the future poet himself. Like so much else in this story it remains a possibility rather than a probability, but it is an intriguing coincidence.

Meanwhile, John Evans went into overdrive as he set out to showcase the intellect and talent of Robert Rose:

> That the genius of the coloured race can be developed as fully in the more refined pursuits of life as the genius in any other, here in the man before us, is the indisputable evidence. What education can do for the European, can be done alike for the Indian, and produce like results. We have had innumerable instances of the truth of this assertion, and it affords us considerable pleasure to be able to notice one of the number, who has not only developed the resources of an extraordinarily cultivated intellect, but has untied with a peculiar strength of judgement of mind, a poetic fancy and no ordinary feeling of magnitude and a literary taste and capacity that has rarely been identified in any of the race with whom by birth he is associated. We are doubly pleased in being able to introduce the name of Robert Rose here … first because he is identified with Lancashire, and next, and more important, it enables us to show that a long vilified race who have called forth scorn and contempt from every hand and side – who have been traduced and slandered in every quarter – who have been coupled with everything savage, illiterate and ignominious – whom surrounded by proper influences, are as capable of attaining an eminence in the realms of mind and genius, as any of the most advanced communities of modern civilisation. Robert Rose is an ornament to his race, and a living contradiction of the contemptible aspersions that have been thrown upon it. He has manifested a mind as fully as much alive to all the exquisite sensations produced by the poetry of nature and art, as is manifested by the inhabitants of

our own, or any other country under the sun. We have had sundry proofs of this in the numerous productions he has given the world. We have had evidence of his refined taste, clear judgement, inventive genius, gentle sensations, powerful conceptions, and clear and easy manner of expressing all his sensations and emotions. And in all this we have experienced extreme pleasure, both in the ability manifested and in consideration of the party from whom they emanated. It is in considering the race from which Mr Rose springs that adds very materially to the value of his productions; and no one giving them a perusal can refrain from acknowledging him to be a somewhat wonderful man.

Chapter Three

'There are millions with warm hearts that dare to break oppression's chains...'

Robert Rose seems to have made no secret of the fact that he had a private income of £300 (worth nearly £21,000 in 2024) per year so he did not need to work, but he wanted to train 'in business'. His 'private means' represented a considerable sum and his hospitable nature was what many remembered about him, so it is tempting to wonder if, in the lonely hours of the night time, he was trying to buy himself friendship. The reason for his receiving such a sum, or from whom, is not known, but it could have been guilt on the part of his father and/or paternal family; simple philanthropy; or perhaps a bribe for keeping quiet about his true origins. Alternatively, it might just have been because his father did not have a legitimate son and was unlikely to do so because he was terminally ill. From what is known of Robert Rose, his character, and his life, his private income is extremely unlikely to have been a bribe. Someone somewhere cared, but not enough to allow him a full West Indian childhood or to keep in touch with his mother. The separation, knowing that she might never see him again, must have broken her heart, although she may have been willing let him go for the sake of a better life for him, in the same way and for the same reasons that Leonardo da Vinci's mother let Leonardo, aged 7, go to his father for his education, training and work. However, that is twenty-first century psychology talking. In the early nineteenth century Rose's removal to a supposedly 'civilised and advanced country' for education, training and well-paid work, plus a handsome 'private income' allowance, would have been seen as the ultimate grand gesture of a father towards his offspring. An unusual one as well, since very few 'persons of colour' had 'private means'.

Who was Robert Rose's 'sponsor' and why? Rose never named him except to say it was a Liverpool MP. This may have been a gentle form of teasing because there were only three abolitionist MPs in Liverpool during the relevant period, all of whom were Whigs (the nineteenth-century equivalent of the twentieth-century Liberal Party) all of whom knew, or knew of, Robert Rose, and, coincidentally, all of whom wrote poetry at some point. It is a reflection, so often lamented in modern detective fiction and fact, that the police can have multiple suspects in a case and, while they may be certain who the real culprit is, they cannot prove it.

The most likely candidate would have been William Ewart, Whig MP for Liverpool (1830–7) after whom the Prime Minister William Ewart Gladstone was named. The Gladstone family had strong links with Scotland, which might explain the choice of Green Row Academy for the young Rose, if indeed he ever attended that school, but Sir John Gladstone (William Gladstone's father) was one of the largest slave holders in the West Indies and passionately in favour of slavery. Ewart was an equally passionate abolitionist. He knew Robert Rose personally and was a great fan of his poetry. However, William Ewart was not born until 1798, which meant that he was still a young child when Robert Rose was born. However, Rose did not come to England before c.1812, when he would have been around 7 years of age, and he was unlikely to have received a private income before his late teens or early twenties. Although Ewart was not particularly wealthy in his youth, he could certainly have acted as an intermediary for the real sponsor.

There were two other possible candidates. The first one was William Roscoe (1753–1831) who was born at Mount Pleasant in Liverpool and became a Whig MP for the city for a year in 1806–7.

He was very much against the slave trade and voted for abolition in 1806. He was a lawyer with over twenty years' experience (so he would have known about trusts or other means of providing Rose with a regular income), a banker, an historian, a botanist who helped to create the Liverpool Botanic Garden (originally near Mount Pleasant), and a writer who published several books on botany and history, as well as *The Butterfly's Ball and the Grasshopper's Feast*. He also wrote pamphlets, including one on African slavery, and a number of poems, one entitled simply 'Mount Pleasant'. When he died in 1831 he was buried in the Unitarian graveyard at Mount Pleasant. Two of his children became poets and his grandson, Henry Enfield Roscoe, became a distinguished chemist who married Lucy Potter, the aunt of internationally acclaimed children's author Beatrix Potter.

The second, and possibly more likely candidate, would have been Henry Brougham, 1st Baron Brougham and Vaux, born in Edinburgh in 1778, so he would have been in the same age group as Rose's parents. Brougham was brought up in Edinburgh and became a passionate abolitionist and a Whig MP – although not for Liverpool, his family lived in the city. Lord Brougham, who was said to have been rather unreliable and arrogant, his 'genius and eloquence' marred by bad judgement, was a Whig Member of Parliament who represented Camelford 1810–12; Winchelsea 1815–30; and Knaresborough for six months in 1830. He was later appointed to a peerage and became Lord High Chancellor of Britain 1830–4 under Earl Grey's ministry. In 1806 he became a staunch and passionate supporter for the abolition of slavery and remained so until his death in 1868. Evans stated that Rose spent some time at a London academy before he went to Green Row. This statement is uncorroborated anywhere else, but, if true, it might strengthen the case for Lord Brougham being Rose's mystery sponsor. Brougham was a well-educated man who wrote on such diverse subjects as maths, politics, surgery, colonial policy and poetry; and he was instrumental in getting the 1832 Reform Act and the 1833 Abolition of Slavery in the West Indies Act passed into law.

It was also at a dinner held in Brougham's honour that Robert Rose first came to notice in the public consciousness with his impassioned speech on abolition and emancipation.

Apart from the three Whig MPs, the other Liverpool MPs during this time were quite right-wing Conservative, and all were strongly in favour of slavery, so it was extremely unlikely that they would have sponsored Rose or any other person of mixed race. However, to quote Arthur Conan Doyle's Sherlock Holmes: 'once you eliminate the impossible, whatever remains, no matter how improbable, must be the truth'. Unlikely though it might be, there is the possibility that a Conservative MP did sponsor Rose as a favour to a friend or colleague. That would certainly be a motive for his being coy about his sponsor. However, there is absolutely no evidence to link any of the relevant Conservative MPs of the time with either the West Indies or with Robert Rose. These MPs included Isaac Gascoyne (Liverpool MP 1796–1830); Dudley Ryder (Liverpool MP 1831–42); Banastre Tarleton (Liverpool MP 1790–6; 1807); George Canning (Liverpool MP 1812); William Huskisson (Liverpool MP 1823). The only one who had any connection with the West Indies, although he never went there, was Banastre Tarleton, whose father John (1718–73) prospered in the West Indian sugar trade and managed slaving vessels which carried human cargoes of slaves. Therefore, on this occasion, it would seem that Sherlock Holmes was wrong.

It is tempting to wonder if it was an MP from another constituency or even an MP at all. Whitehaven, where Rose was said to have first landed in Britain, was not created as a parliamentary constituency until 1832, and in any case it was a deeply Conservative area in the nineteenth century. The only other explanation, knowing Rose's love of playing on words and his insistence on being coy, is that MP stood for something other than Member of Parliament. There was no police force at that time but it could have been a member of a religious or other society. However the truth, as perhaps Robert Rose intended, is unlikely to ever be known.

Chapter Four

'...and nations cry aloud "we will be free!"'

On 20 July 1835 a public dinner was held in Lord Brougham's honour at the Amphitheatre in Liverpool to commemorate the laying of the foundation stone for a new Mechanics' Institute. Robert Rose, a keen lifelong supporter of Mechanics' Institutes, which provided further education for all via evening classes, was one of the guests.

Speaking of slavery, Brougham declared that 'the slave is as fit for his freedom as any English peasant, aye or any Lord I now address … I demand his rights! I demand his liberty without stint … I demand your brother be no longer trampled upon as your slave.'

After Lord Brougham had finished giving his speech condemning slavery at the dinner, a toast was given to 'civil and religious liberty all over the world'.

Emboldened perhaps by the passion of someone who spoke so eloquently on the subject which mattered the most to him, it was at this point that Robert Rose first peeped through the curtains of history. His olive skin glowed in the lamp light and the warmth of the July evening as he stood to address the assembly with an impassioned speech in favour of the abolition of slavery and emancipation of slaves; particularly those of the West Indies, where the 1833 Act had come into force during the summer of 1834. He was perhaps a little too verbose for modern tastes, and, in fact, for some of those from his own time, but his message was clear:

> I look round me, and I could not refrain from asking myself 'where are *my* countrymen?' Alas! They have

been groaning under a bondage similar to that in olden times inflicted by the task masters of Egypt; and of them, I *alone* am here, a free-born man, to express for them their deep obligations to him [Lord Brougham] and to you. This pleasing task has devolved on me *alone*, and this is, indeed, the proudest hour of my life, when I am so specially favoured above them as to have it in my power personally to thank their benefactors, among the foremost and most generous of whom how happy I am to recognise HENRY LORD BROUGHAM.

Rose then becomes rather fulsome and verbose in his justification of the abolition of slavery, which he realises has been resisted by many, and, after the fashion of the times, he goes into overdrive, quite keen not to offend, but at the same time to make his point forcefully:

I ween, there can be no candid or substantial objection raised, as universality is its basis, and in it is engendered and embodied everything that is beauteous or holy in religion … that is noble or pure in morality … charity and good will to all men; and lean this individual's ideas one way, or that individual's another; be the reasoning facilities ever so much debased, enervated, or prostituted; let all the sophisms which have ever been adduced, be started against it in a mighty concatenation of encyclopaedia array; still this grand principle, on which no eloquence can fully enough expatiate, stands, in its condensed strength as on a rock of ages, which is too firmly fixed to be cast asunder, or in the least particle shaken, by the conflicting discords of mankind: it flows from the everlasting fountain of justice and mercy; rising superior in all lowly distinctions; it directly appeals to the Godhead and thence to the natural and ever durable laws between man and man; and by it, through it, and for it, everything in this sublunary sphere lives, moves, and hath its being: it is to be found most active in this gem of the earth, this queen of the ocean; for 'Tis liberty that crowns Britannia's isle, and makes her barren rocks and her bleak mountains smile.

The audience approved and applauded these sentiments and Rose continued:

I now wish to draw your thoughts to the *degraded* state in which my countrymen have been held (having been ... debarred all the advantageous effects of education and rational liberty) ... comparing it to their present happier condition, and all the benefits they now enjoy ... that through your interposition ... those sufferers who have toiled and toiled through years of pain and misery, those whose bread of affliction hath been steeped alas in the bitter cup of sorrow, those who have far too long been compelled to drink the turbid waters of cool mockery, and whose fate it hath been to be tormented by the scorpion stings of unfeeling and ruffian scorn are now elevated in the scale of social being. They have long laboured by the sweat of their brow for what compensation? Blows, stripes and the ignominious burdens imposed on them by self-made traffickers in human flesh, although their Christianity ... informs them that the almighty and omniscient Ruler, who cares for the smallest insect in his extended works, has made of one blood all the nations on earth.

He sees with equal eye, as God of all,
A hero perish, or a sparrow fall.

> But this ... Divine Providence hath been wickedly
> defeated by demons in human shape ... reckless of
> plaintive cries ... to the supernal realms of justice ...
> Have not my countrymen been treated worse than
> felons, or dogs, or reptiles crawling upon the face of
> the earth? Have they not been galled, jaded ... torn
> from the bosom of their families ... never again to
> view the well-known fields where ... they sported in
> all the innocence of boyhood ... doomed to drag out, in
> strict companionship with melancholy, oft approaching
> despair, their severe pittance of existence, until death
> itself ... hath been hailed by them with rapture ... but,
> thank God, their chains have been struck from them! ...
> They are endowed with the same rights, and gifted with
> the same privileges in the creation, in common with all.

After likening abolition to a magic wand waving away gloom and despondency and revitalising everyone, Rose emphasised the gratitude for and benefits of abolition once more.

Some points were considered a little too much for his audience and Rose recognised this fact: 'It may be considered that I have gone too far,' he said, continuing with assurances that the freed slaves were truly grateful but, he insisted:

> the march of intellect is greater than the march of armies,
> and England has with rapid strides outstripped other
> countries in the race of glory; and how can she fail
> when she can boast of such master-spirits as a Henry
> Brougham ... and when we glance at Liverpool, we survey
> with gratitude the public conduct of such personages.

He thanked local dignitaries and then apologised for trespassing on so much of the audience's time, admitting it was his first time of public speaking, but he continued to lavish more praise on Lord Brougham and to emphasise the importance of abolition and emancipation. Despite some heckling towards the end, his speech was generally well received, and it was proposed by several attendees that the text should be printed and sold – to which Rose agreed, providing the proceeds went to charity. Lord Brougham had had to leave the meeting after his own speech and so he did not hear Rose speak, which was considered by those present to be a great shame. Although Rose was jeered by some Americans at the public dinner for suggesting people of colour were equal to any other people, he pleaded for immediate abolition and emancipation; his pleas mainly fell on deaf ears. The conditions, abuse and ill treatment of slaves continued until final abolition in the West Indies in 1838; although abolition did not come in America until the passing of the 13th Amendment in December 1865. Rose published the speech in pamphlet form and it sold well, but nothing really changed as a result.

A reporter from the *Liverpool Standard* wrote an excellent article on the more emotional part of Rose's speech:

SPEECH OF MR ROBERT ROSE AT THE BROUGHAM DINNER, LIVERPOOL.

We should have forgotten by this time that so great a man as Lord Brougham had some month or two since dined at the Amphitheatre, if as great, if not a greater orator, Mr Robert Rose, a gentleman of colour, had not published a speech which he delivered on that occasion to the select few who had nerve enough to remain some hours after the chairman had vacated the chair, and Mr James Aiken had undertaken to supply his place. 'Civil and religious liberty all over the world' – to which 'everywhere else', we presume, was added by the patriots and philanthropists then and there present — was the toast to which the 'gentleman of colour' responded, and that he performed his part bravely the following extract will show. 'Even as some time-honoured edifice, glittering with the mellow radiance of vernal splendour, so hath the munificence of your benevolence imparted hallowed brilliance to a land where gloom was hovering, which seemed bereft of hope, and consigned to wretchedness, adding, as if with a wand of magic, new features to the scene. In as much as 'that land, originally so like a garden of Eden, which should never have been trampled on by an oppressor, is now repeopled with new forms, as it were, with cheerful tones and merry countenances; —and I think, nay, I am sure— that they will never, never prove themselves unworthy of your kindness. (Cheers.) They breathe in free air;–(Does Mr Rose here allude to the blacks of St Domingo?)—they walk erect,—they feel,—they reason,—(laughter,)— they can reason,—(laughter,)—they move with limbs— unshackled and with brow undaunted,—they sustain the sacred dignity or humanity,—they exult in the glad consciousness of liberty! and, as they can now do—what the animals or wild beasts of the woods could always do—(laughter)—roam at large over the ground; as they pace it with buoyant steps, I have no doubt they can discover that the herbs of the field, and the flowers of the garden flourish for them as well as for others of the human species, (laughter,) and show me the wretch who dares to say they display no signs of intellect and ought not to experience the advantages of knowledge. (Interruption.) Who is he, and where is he who dares to hazard such an abominable assertion? Let him stand forward! I am here to answer him. (Cries of 'Personal'.) Gracious heavens! is he so wedded to his lamentable dullness, or is he so immersed in his own filthy selfishness, (cries of 'Personal',) as to be dead to all human sympathy? Do but point him out to me. (Cries of 'Stop', and partial hissing.) Some of you may hiss, like serpents, but you do not possess the serpent's sting. (Laughter.) I have not been personal intentionally, but 'the guilty flee when no man pursues'. (Loud laughter.) In another part of his speech the gentleman of colour said, 'What heart doth not bound with inward pleasure, what heart doth not feel ennobled with the idea that it can identify itself as palpitating to him who exists in the same age as Henry Lord Brougham.' (Enthusiastic cheers.) The subjoined note is appended to Mr Rose's speech, and explains the irreverent and unseemly interruptions which he had to contend against: 'The members, of a committee of West Indians, selected for the publication of the foregoing speech, think it their duty to remark, that a full report of it is rather injured, from the interruptions which Mr Rose experienced; and it is their wish, in publishing this, to do him justice, as far as possible, under existing circumstances, in the eyes of the public and of his countrymen, to whom copies of it will be transmitted. The annoyance which he received, and which they exceedingly regret should have occurred, proceeded from a very few Americans, who were the only persons who appeared to evince no sympathy with the object which he had in view. This they consider due to him to state, as many casual observers might be disposed to infer that he trespassed too long on the attention of the meeting. When attending on him to communicate their project, he kindly offered to correct the report, and likewise expressed a desire that the proceeds arising from its sale should be appropriated to charitable purposes – We would recommend Mr Rose to lose no time in sailing for Charleston, U.S.; so florid a speaker will be of immense advantage to the cause of 'civil and religious liberty' in the land of the free'.

[*Liverpool Standard and General Commercial Advertiser*, 18 September 1835]

About a month later, seemingly on the strength of his speech at Lord Brougham's dinner, a public dinner was held for Robert Rose himself which was reported by the *Liverpool Albion*:

> **DINNER GIVEN TO MR ROBERT ROSE. —On** Monday evening a dinner was given to Mr Robert Rose, at the Globe Coffee-house, by the friends and members of the Theoretic Society of this town. The speech which he delivered on the occasion, and which lasted an hour and five minutes, gave very general satisfaction. From a Correspondent. ROBERT ROSE.
>
> [*Liverpool Albion*, 19 October 1835]

For his part, Robert Rose was also anxious that William Ewart should receive his share of the credit in the fight for abolition, and later that autumn applauded efforts to have a dinner held in William Ewart's honour. He wrote in answer to a letter he saw on this subject in the *Liverpool Mercury*:

> **To THE EDITOR OF THE LIVERPOOL MERCURY.**
> I read with pleasure the remarks of a correspondent of yours, last week, urging the Reformers to invite our worthy representative Mr Ewart, to a public dinner. I therefore hasten, as I could not take a more favourable opportunity, to submit to your perusal some letters from that gentleman to a Mr Ashley of this town, as they may serve, among numerous other instances to observe the unremitting attention of our respected Member to the welfare of his constituents. Each of his letters, besides the business-like manner and substance of them, being written in Immediate answer to the former gentleman's application relative to a customary

Trinity-House-pension, awarded to superannuated captains, especially at a time when his parliamentary duties and avocations must have peculiarly pressed upon him. It may, certainly, be deemed almost superfluous to advance this additional proof of his diligence and care, but in this instance, I flatter myself it will answer two purposes. In such traits as this we more distinctly and definitely can ascertain the true, though fainter traces of a public character, when the eyes of the multitude are not directed towards it; and, secondly, Mr Ashley placed the letters in my hands, very properly wishing Mr Ewart's attention to him, to be made known, and his thanks to be thus publicly given to him. And, I now acknowledge that it affords me much satisfaction to be the humble instrument of his so doing. I have now only have to point heartily with all of the Reformers, who only want a beginning to it, I, in hoping we may, ere long, testify our gratitude to Mr Ewart in a more substantial manner than empty thanks, by inviting him to a public dinner.

Yours, ROBERT ROSE.

[*Liverpool Mercury*, Friday, 6 November 1835]

There is a curious postscript to Robert Rose's speech. Although given at a public dinner in Liverpool, subsequently published by public request, then reprinted, its author a Black person born into a world of slavery, there is no copy of this speech available on public access anywhere in the United Kingdom. The only known copy in Britain is held by Goldsmith's Library in London – but it is not available to the public. Although the speech was first given nearly 200 years ago there is still much in it that is relevant today. Consequently, a full version has been published as an appendix to this book courtesy of the National Library of Australia, based in Canberra.

Chapter Five

'Reason proved our strength...'

To give such a speech Robert Rose must have been actively involved, if not immersed, in the whole subject of slavery and anti-slavery, so it might have been expected that he would write on the subject to the local newspapers, of which he became so fond during his poetry writing career, but if he did, there is no trace remaining.

At this time child labour was rife in England and it was the scandal of Europe. A quarter of the mining workforce and a third of the workforce in the mills were made up of children, some as young as 5. By 1833 children accounted for two thirds of all textile workers and children under the age of 13 accounted for up to 20 per cent of all workers in the cotton, wool, flax and silk mills. Ironically, the child slaves of America worked shorter hours in better conditions than the child workers in England. Equally ironic is the fact that in 1833, along with the Abolition of Slavery in the West Indies Act, the Factories Act 1833 was also passed, banning children under 9 from working. Initially, this was ignored on quite a wide scale and working children of 6 or 7 remained fairly common until the 1840s. The doctor who looked after children at Quarry Bank Mill, near Styal on the Cheshire border, was the uncle of Elizabeth Gaskell and he often took her with him on his rounds. His treatment book has survived and with it the entries of the medical problems and dispensed remedies (which included live leeches for blood-letting) for child workers at Quarry Bank Mill from the age of 7 upwards). Elizabeth Gaskell was horrified and in her first novel (*Mary Barton*, 1848) highlighted the dreadful social imbalances of the time. Shunting between Liverpool and Manchester, cities at the heart of this situation, Rose could not fail to have been aware of the issues of child labour which did not begin to be resolved until the passing of the Ten Hours Act in 1847, restricting those under 18 to a maximum ten-hour working day. However, Rose seems to have taken care not to mention anything about the situation of child workers in Britain, keeping strictly to the slavery inflicted on people of colour. He was intelligent enough to realise it was a subject too close to home for the English and there were too many vested interests locally in Liverpool and Manchester to whom it would cause serious offence. The West Indies were at a sufficient distance and, in any case, many of the slave owners there were Scottish and not Lancastrian. Besides, it could be argued that in theory, British children were free to leave or change employment and habitation without penalty. In practice this was not the case at all. Children had to sign to say they would complete a number of years in 'apprenticeship'. If they ran away they were caught, whipped and sometimes taken before the courts.

Despite the success of his eloquent, if lengthy speech, on the abolition of slavery and emancipation of slaves, it subsequently became obvious that 1835 was a catalyst for Robert Rose. It was clear that he had harboured dreams of returning to his homeland, the land of his birth, and it was equally clear that something happened to destroy that dream, at least temporarily. Rose himself gives no verbal clue and few poetic clues, but actions can speak louder than words and his subsequent actions demonstrate that events in the latter 1830s broke his spirit, despite the recent abolition of slavery in the West Indies. The most likely initial explanation is that freed West Indian slaves were to undergo a compulsory five-year 'apprenticeship' to 'prepare slaves to assume the duties of freemen' and to educate them in literacy; in practice, it was simply an extension of their slavery, so that real abolition and emancipation would not occur before at least 1838. However, from 1838 onwards, this was followed by the 'indenture system', a method by which immigrants from the by then subjugated and British-controlled Indian sub-continent were paid an extremely low basic wage for a fifty-hour week on a five-year contract to work in British Guiana doing the work of the former slaves. By 1838 over 230,000 indentured labourers had arrived in British Guiana from the Indian sub-continent to work in the sugar industry, but, ironically, they were resented by the newly freed African slaves. As David Olusoga writes in 'Cotton Capital' (*The Guardian*, April 2023: 'while former slave owners were awarded … compensation for their "loss of human property" those they had enslaved got nothing … emancipation left them landless, homeless … and destitute'. No one would offer them a job now that their work had to be paid for, no matter how lowly the pay.

According to Olusoga, *Uncle Tom's Cabin* (Harriet Beecher Stowe) was published in 1852 'as a powerful denouncement of the cruelties of American slavery', which referred mainly to the North American cotton slaves but was equally true for the South American cotton, coffee and sugar plantation slaves. In 1859, just ten years after Rose's death, Sarah Parker Remond, a mixed-race African-American abolitionist, in a lecture at the Manchester Athenaeum (presently Manchester Art Gallery) stated: 'when I walk through the streets of Manchester and meet load after load of cotton I think of those cotton plantations on which was grown millions of dollars worth of cotton … and I remember that not one per cent of that money ever reached the hands of the labourers'. Liverpool had been the main port for the Atlantic slave trade and for cotton imports, but it was the 'dark satanic mills' of Manchester which turned the raw cotton into goods worth millions that were exported all over the world – although fortunes were only made for comparatively few people.

Racism, of course, was rife. There was an almost automatic disrespect for those whose skins were brown or black, or for anyone who did not meet Aryan ideals. Many regarded them as sub-human and to be treated on a par with animals. In fact, the dogs often got better treatment on the plantations than the slaves and they were certainly never subjected to the prolonged, sometimes daily, whippings. It was also a natural assumption that the brains of black and brown-skinned people were inferior by definition. However, the main support for slaves came in fact from the cotton mill workers, who worked a minimum of sixty hour weeks for 15 shillings (75 pence, worth the equivalent of about £46 in current values). The cotton workers of the Manchester mills saw themselves and others as equal, regardless of skin colour, and consequently they were as one with the slave plantation workers of America. They later supported the slaves during the American Civil War – although at the cost of their own livelihoods.

The names by which people of colour were known in the nineteenth century are fortunately illegal today, but Robert Rose took his own stand against racism by absolutely insisting on being known as 'the Bard of Colour' from the late 1830s until his death. Rose suffered from racism just the same as everyone else with his skin colour, but because he was possessed of 'private means' and an hospitable personality, he escaped some of the worst abuse – although even his own close literary friends teased him. When he failed to complete what was supposed to be the major work of his life, an epic poem about 'The Ocean', two of his friends from the Sun Inn Poets, John Critchley Prince and John Bolton Rogerson, placed the following advertisement in the newspapers of the day which read: 'Shortly will be published The Ocean – a mystery. By A. Black, London; Blackwood, Glasgow; Blackie, Edinburgh: Black.'

Rose laughed and said he didn't mind. He was intelligent and perceptive enough to know that putting a smile on his face and acts of bonhomie were his best form of protection – but he did mind. Dreadfully. And his pain can be heard in his poetry.

In his pre-Christmas offering to William Ewart MP a few months after his speech at Lord Brougham's dinner in Liverpool, his anguish at the plight of slaves in general, and his beloved West Indies in particular, spills over; his anger and pain pouring out onto the page.

It is an old cliché that the pen is mightier than the sword but in this case it is actually true, the cry for justice and an end to suffering echoing across the years:

REFORM, DEDICATED, BY PERMISSION, TO WM. EWART, ESQ., M.P.

Ah, who can witness what our chiefs have done
Without confiding in what yet will be?
'Tis Freedom tells her battles will be won,
And nations cry aloud 'We will be free!'
For souls like thine now aid our glorious cause,
And baffle the dark arts of wily foes.
We are not slow, for on our side the laws
And Reason prove our strength, will hurl down those
Who proudly stand in selfishness apart,
And turn deaf ears to Misery's plaintive tale;
But thousands, millions, now indignant start
Driving them onward, as the rushing gale
Sweeps the vile dust along, strike with despair
The loathsome monster, writhing Tyranny.
AY, there are millions with warm hearts that dare
To break Oppression's chains or nobly die.
The few who have no sympathies to give,
Who crouch unto the earth and cannot feel,
The 'warrior faction' who ignobly live,
With hearts as cold as is the murderer's steel,
Shrink in dismay, to hear a nation's groan,
And voices loud appealing to the throne !
Dec. 8, 1835. ROBERT ROSE.

Former slave owners were able to claim huge compensation for their lost slaves (so huge that the compensations were not fully paid off until 2015), while the slaves and their descendants got absolutely nothing, and many were reduced to penury. The sheer injustice of this situation, plus the realisation that his skin colour was always going to be a problem, especially if he wanted to be involved in commercial activities and trading, or, indeed, in any business, between Britain and the West Indies, may finally have helped to break Rose's spirit. If he had hoped to return to Berbice with his knowledge and his connections in Liverpool to help his fellow countrymen enter the more profitable world of the white man, then this dream now lay in tatters, at least so far as Rose was concerned, because it had become abundantly clear to him that persons of colour would always be considered as inferior, fit only for menial work, and he felt that he would never be accepted or taken seriously in any other capacity by white colleagues. Rose was not stupid and by this time he would have worked out that his 'private means' would have come from the rich profits gained from using unpaid labour by 'persons of colour'. This realisation would have stung, and it might well have been a turning point for him, because it was in 1835 that he first began to write poetry. By now, although he longed for his own country, Rose also feared that it may have changed beyond recognition for him. Was it this fear that made him delay his return further?

> Can I forget where first I hailed the light?
> Land of my birth! Thy shores I long to tread.
> In thought my mother's voice chides dull delay
> And lures me to my home, that long lost scene
> But if again my footsteps there may stray
> Say, shall I find it as it once hath been…

Chapter Six

'Is beauty bound to colour, shape or air? No. God created all his offspring fair'

Sometime, during the latter 1830s, or perhaps even as late as 1841/2, Robert Rose left Liverpool to live in Manchester. He may have spent the later 1830s commuting between the two cities, his permanent home based in Liverpool, and using temporary addresses in Manchester. The reasons are complex but, in many ways, it was a surprising choice. He loved the sea. He said that the ocean made him feel closer to his homeland and Liverpool was the port from which he had intended to return to his homeland. He had made a life for himself in the city, and he knew people there. The local papers were publishing some of his poems, although there was sometimes a little criticism of his style which seemed to upset and offend him. His instinct for a change of scenery was understandable. His choice of new scenery was not so understandable. If he felt uncomfortable in Liverpool he could have gone anywhere, especially as he had no need to find work. Why Manchester and how would he adapt to life there? Rose continued to sell his work to Liverpool newspapers and to maintain links with Liverpool. His choice may have been influenced the fact that in 1830 the world's 'first inter-urban rail link' between Liverpool and Manchester was built which would have made travelling to Manchester comparatively easy and simple. The inaugural journey took place on 15 September 1830 and consisted of eight trains, including the Rocket. Robert Rose may very well have been one of those who made that initial trip because he would have been intrigued and had the means to pay for a journey. He may also have been considering regular travel to Manchester anyway because that city had an emerging arts and cultural scene which was superior to Liverpool and this had aroused his curiosity.

Manchester, however, was very different from Liverpool. There was no fresh sea air to offset the choking emissions from the mills and manufactories. The Manchester Ship Canal had yet to be built so there were no ocean-going ships or proper docks, and the city was gloomier and darker than Liverpool in many ways. In 1835 Alexis de Tocqueville had written of Manchester:

> A sort of black smoke covers the city. The sun seen through it is a disc without rays. Under this half daylight 300,000 human beings are ceaselessly at work. A thousand noises disturb this damp, dark labyrinth, but they are not at all the ordinary sounds one hears in great cities. The footsteps of a busy crowd, the crunching wheels of machinery, the shriek of steam from boilers, the regular beat of the looms, the heavy rumble of carts, those are the noises from which you can never escape in the sombre half-light of these streets. From this foul drain the greatest stream of human industry flows out to fertilise the whole world. From this filthy sewer pure gold flows. Here humanity attains its most complete development and its most brutish; here civilisation works its miracles, and civilised man is turned back almost into a savage.

Friedrich Engels followed this in 1844 with:

> Such is the Old Town of Manchester it is far from black enough to convey a true impression of the filth, ruin, and uninhabitableness, the defiance of all considerations

of cleanliness, ventilation, and health. True, this is the Old Town, and the people of Manchester emphasise the fact whenever anyone mentions to them the frightful condition of this Hell upon Earth; but what does that prove? Everything which here arouses horror and indignation is of recent origin, belongs to the industrial epoch.

Why did Robert Rose choose to live in this unattractive sounding city? The answer almost certainly lies in his career change from learning about business and its methods to writing poetry. Although never officially acknowledged, Manchester had a much stronger cultural and literary scene than Liverpool. The new railway offered a simple and comparatively easy connection between the two cities. It is known that Rose became a frequent visitor to Chetham's Library in Manchester, often with a girl on his arm. Although the medieval buildings of Chetham's date back to 1421, Chetham's Library was established in 1653 and is the oldest free public reference library in the English-speaking world. Rose was fond of Chetham's and the library holds his only known surviving notebook, as well as the two pamphlets of poetry which he published; one containing poems on the 'Coronation of Queen Victoria' and the benefits of 'Sunday Schools', the other a poem simply entitled 'The Bazaar'. Karl Marx and Friedrich Engels worked together in a small alcove off the main reading room in Chetham's Library during the latter 1840s and published their Communist Manifesto in 1848. Tempting to wonder if Robert Rose met either of them, but, if he did, it is almost certain he would have written a poem about it. He also frequented the Portico Library, an independent subscription library, with a splendid central glass dome, built 1802–6, on Mosley Street, which had open fires and restaurant facilities, then as now. The Portico has changed little since 1806 and to sit by a real fire in the old-fashioned members lounge with its deep armchairs and rickety floor-to-ceiling dark wooden bookshelves is to have pretty much the same experience as Robert Rose would have had in the mid-nineteenth century.

Another of the many unknowns about Robert Rose is where he wrote his poetry. Most likely in the companionable comfort of Chetham's Library or the Portico, but also maybe in his own lodgings. At least two addresses for him (Oxford Street in Manchester and St Stephen's Street across the river in Salford) are verifiable, and it is known that he sometimes used the address of Richard Cobden (1804–61), a radical Liberal and an advocate of free trade who opposed the hated Corn Laws. These deeply unpopular laws kept the price of corn artificially high after the Battle of Waterloo in 1815 and ensured that consumers, not producers, suffered economically. Cobden lived at Cobden House, 19 Quay Street, Manchester – a house that subsequently became the first home of Owens College, the foundation of the Victoria University of Manchester. Although Rose continued to have much of his work published in Liverpool newspapers, for which he might well have retained an interest in Helen Rose's address on Mount Pleasant, if indeed that Robert Rose and the poet were the same person, he nevertheless turned his attention towards the opportunities Manchester might have to offer.

Thomas de Quincey, a Manchester writer and fervent abolitionist of slavery, born in 1785, had published his renowned *Confessions of an English Opium Eater* in 1821, but according to Dr Deborah Woodman in *The Story of Manchester*, there was also a group of writers 'representing a vibrant and artistic working-class culture' who were excluded from the mainstream literary scene solely on account of their class, not their talents. Class has long been a British obsession and as recently as the mid-twentieth century it was still not the 'done thing' for people to marry, or, in some cases, even to consort socially, outside their class. Amazingly, in the twenty-first century, there are still aristocratic families who cling to the idea of not marrying below one's station in life. Robert Rose's chief problem, of course, was his skin colour. Class did not even come into the equation. He was considered Black, so there was nothing else to be said. However, he could identify and deal with exclusion at many levels, and he hoped that there would be openings for him.

In British Guiana by the 1820s around 40 per cent of slaves were of African descent and around 40 per cent were of Native American Indian descent, so it was not considered absolutely certain to which group Rose's ancestors belonged. The very few existing descriptions of him refer to his 'olive skin', which indicated that he could have had West Indian, rather than African, origins. The indigenous inhabitants of what would become British Guiana were Amerindian people who would have physically resembled North American Native American Indians. Rose himself says his mother was a free woman, not a slave, so it was possible she could have been Amerindian; and John Evans refers to him as Indian, although this may well refer to the West Indian islands of the Caribbean. However, Rose always continued to refer to himself as a Creole, which indicated that his mother was African, not Indian. About this time Rose began calling himself the Laureate of the Western Isles. Rose had always liked to play on words and this may have been a discreet but meaningful reference to his unacknowledged paternal family. He had a Scottish name. Highlanders from the Ross and Cromarty areas played a large part in owning and managing the sugar plantations of the West Indies and the name Rose was common among them. The islands off the western Scottish coast opposite Ross and Cromarty, the Inner and Outer Hebrides, are known as the Western Isles. In the area of the Caribbean the islands of the West Indies, just off the coast of South America, are also known as the Western Isles. Robert Rose had already freely admitted that he was West Indian and he would have enjoyed this particular play on words. It was also a way for him to acknowledge the country he considered his home country on the same level as his adopted country which, at that time, was considered to be far superior to British Guiana.

Rose had doubtless heard of a writer's circle headed by John Critchley Prince, a former reed maker and factory worker who subsequently ran a small bookshop situated opposite the Sun Inn on Long Millgate, close to Chetham's Library. Prince had established a group known as the Sun Inn Poets who met regularly at the Long Millgate pub of the same name. Long Millgate was, as its name suggests, a long road, winding and cobbled, in the heart of Manchester, near Chetham's School of Music. Today a wide sloping green and the Urbis Football Museum stand on the former site of Long Millgate and its iconic pub, the Sun Inn. It takes an effort of imagination to conjure up the crooked building of medieval timbers to which Robert Rose gravitated, now replaced by lawns and a water feature. The Sun Inn Poets were originally a group of twelve whose numbers grew to fifty and included such well-known northern writers as Samuel Bamford, John Bolton Rogerson, Charles Swain, Isabella Varley (later Mrs G. Linnaeus Banks who wrote *The Manchester Man*), Richard Wright Proctor and Elijah Ridings.

The Sun Inn Poets, who were mainly working-class poets, were centred around John Critchley Prince, but much of the administrative work was done by John Bolton Rogerson (chairman) and Robert Rose. Prince appears to have welcomed Robert Rose because by 1841 Rose was their vice chairman – the same year in which they established the Lancashire Literary Association. There was some banter about his colour but he appeared to take it in the spirit in which it was intended, at least on the surface. He seemed to have found a niche for himself and he was happy with it. However, it may have secretly rankled with him, for it was around 1840–1 that he had begun styling himself the Bard of Colour, by which epithet he was known for the rest of his life, as well the Laureate of the Western Isles. Rose always enjoyed a play on words and creating a kind of mystique about himself. It is very open to question as to whether he actually knew exactly who his paternal family were, but he knew the name of Rose was prevalent in both Berbice, on the shores of the Caribbean, and in the Scottish Highlands, the home of many of the Caribbean plantation owners, and he would have known that the Western Isles in Britain referred to the Inner and Outer Hebrides off the western coast of the Scottish Highlands. He would have known as well that the islands of the Caribbean off the coast of Guiana, the country of which Berbice was a part, were also known as the Western Isles. That double entendre would have suited Rose perfectly.

John Evans wrote about Robert Rose, and the reason for his self-styling as the Bard of Colour, in the *Nottingham and Newark Mercury* on 15 June 1849:

> The Bard of Colour [as Rose referred to himself] I have known for some eight or ten years past, and in common justice to him, consider that he has peculiar claims upon your esteem and notice, both in respect of his private worth, and his literary acquirements and Indian origins. In good fellowship you may rarely meet with a foreigner more thoroughly identified with our own national character, perfectly in unison with its most amiable amenities of domestic life, a personification of affable, social, courteous frankness, and under his own roof hospitable withal, as one of our best examples of an English gentleman. I state this merely in opposition to a less genial spirit and feeling which is in the ascription of some persons, men of another clime are said to possess. He is a most worthy friend amongst us, open and generous in feeling-generous in spirit-generous in action. In the emotions of the poet, the lyre of Mr Rose has been oft and vigorously strung to soul stirring emotions-he

has spoken eloquently of that slavery which is too monstrous, too hideous for human imaginings, insulting to the creator of the universe, and degrading his earthly likeness. Surely these are subjects for the poet's pen, worthy of being enshrined against the loftiest creations of his genius. The Bard of Colour has boldly anathamatised [*sic*] the oppressors of the human race – the traffickers in blood- the despoilers of freedom; in short, a soul responsive to the truthful power and beauty of the Bard of Sheffield (James Montgomery).

James Montgomery (1771–1854), the self-styled 'Bard of Sheffield', was the son of a Moravian missionary in the city. His parents had left him at school in a Leeds Moravian college when they emigrated to the West Indies, where they died within a year of each other. As an adult he returned to Sheffield, where he lived for the rest of his life. He worked as a journalist and became editor of the *Sheffield Iris*. He also wrote and published hymns and poetry, but was imprisoned twice for writing controversial political articles. In 1809 he wrote a poem simply called 'The West Indies' about the slave trade in the West Indies; and in 1831 he compiled a book about the travels of two Moravian missionaries which contained a chapter on African slaves. Although Montgomery styled himself the 'Bard of Sheffield' he is chiefly known for his hymns. He wrote around 400 hymns, of which about a quarter are still sung today. There is no record that Rose and Montgomery ever met, but Rose would certainly have known of him, and it is tempting to wonder if he copied Montgomery's mode of address when he styled himself the 'Bard of Colour' and 'Bard of the Western Isles'.

Anxious to emphasise the talent of Robert Rose, a talent which was evidently considered most unusual at the time for a person of colour, John Evans was now insistent on gaining full recognition for Rose's poetic talent.

> I trust Mr Rose will proceed in his laudable aspirations; an honour and example to his native (West Indies) land – and an ornament to our own country.

> 'Is beauty bound to colour, shape or air?
> No. God created all his offspring fair.'

With these faithful observations we must fully concur. The genius of a 'bard of colour' has rarely [never] been developed to the same extent. Of course, it is not to be supposed that Mr Rose has attained the *ne plus ultra* of poetic invention, yet we do believe that he is imbued with all the sentiments and emotions of a genuine poetical temperament, and that his expression of the same manifests considerable energy and must be regarded as somewhat wondrous when we consider his birth and extraction. All honour, then, to the 'Bard of the Isles' – for he deserves it! He is one of a class that we shall not meet in our everyday walks and rambles. He is a genuine character, and we rejoice heartily in both himself and his works. We must willingly accord him a niche in the humble temple we are raising, for we are impressed that he fully merits it – 'would it were worthier'. The strains he has sung are elevated and elevating, for they have told of freedom, love, purity and beauty. He has shown himself a lover of freedom in the most enlarged sense, and an enthusiastic devotee at the shrine of everything partaking in the sublime and beautiful in God's universe. Hence Mr Rose must be regarded as one of the most surprising geniuses of the land of his birth; and everyone having had the same means of observing his capacities as we have had, must acknowledge it.

Prejudice over his skin colour, which was prevalent during his lifetime because of slavery and the notion that only white men had 'proper brains', may also have been the reason why Rose took to imbibing more frequently than was strictly necessary for general conviviality. At first this might have gone unnoticed as the group of poets met in a pub and held regular dinners there – but some did notice. At three o'clock in the morning of 7 August 1841, he was attacked on Brazennose Street, near Manchester Town Hall, and robbed of £10 (£604 at 2017 values), which was a lot of ready cash for him to be carrying around. His attacker claimed that Rose had been drunk and that he had merely been trying to help him. Rose, of course, hotly denied it, but the question has to be asked: what was he doing on the streets of Manchester in the middle of the night with so much money on his person? Had he, in modern idiom, been 'flashing his cash'? Perhaps still trying to buy friendship with his hospitality.

On 7 January 1842 a well attended poetry recital took place at the Sun Inn, and following its success a poetry festival was held at the inn on 24 March 1842. Much of the group's poetical output was published in *Bradshaw's Journal*, but in July 1842 Rogerson published the Festival Poetry as 'The Festive Wreath' which it was hoped would herald a new regional school of poetry. Sadly, this did not happen, and it remains the Sun Inn group's sole publishing venture. The Lancashire Literary Association, which had been formed by the group on 28 July 1841, only lasted until 1843 as Prince, the principal figure of the group, Rogerson, and another key member moved away and the momentum was lost. Its aim had been to publish a monthly journal of work by the Sun Inn Poets but this simply did not happen, which would undoubtedly have been a major disappointment for Robert Rose. Although many of the group's former members remained in touch as friends, several turned away from poetry to concentrate on either fiction or journalism and the Sun Inn Poets passed into history.

Chapter Seven

'Since last I wandered by the Mersey's shore...'

When and where in Manchester did Robert Rose live? Information is sketchy. He wrote a letter of protest to the *Manchester Times* on 8 November 1837, about a 'literary attack' on him in the *Liverpool Mail* of 10 October 1837, giving his address as 18 Oxford Street, Manchester. In his book *Some Manchester Streets and their Buildings* (Liverpool UP, 1924), C.H. Reilly dismissed the area of Oxford Street as a bit downmarket with some of the local buildings 'a bad survival of a nuisance period', but he also notes that 'most of the buildings [before Portland Street] have been old domestic ones altered with shops and offices and much damaged in the process'. Today there is a chemist's shop on the site where No.18 might have stood.

Pigot's Directory for Manchester in 1841 lists a mechanic, Robert Rose, living at 2 Hennes Street off Butler Street, which is in the present Northern Quarter. Initially that entry was dismissed, but Rose was quite involved with the Mechanics' Institutes in both Liverpool and Manchester as further education resources, because he believed in the value of universal education for everyone, a point he had made during his speech on emancipation in 1835, and he liked to play on words. It's a possibility. Around this time it is believed that he may also have used Richard Cobden's house, on the corner of Quay Street and Byrom Street, as an address. Cobden was a leader of the Anti-Corn Laws Association until the Corn Laws were repealed in

1846. He was also the Liberal MP for neighbouring Stockport from 1841–7. The house subsequently became Owens College which formed the foundation of the Victoria University of Manchester.

A poem written in 1842 about revisiting Liverpool, and noting changes which had occurred there, indicate that Rose may indeed have left some time beforehand; although he continued to have a fondness for sending his work to Liverpool newspapers. It is possible that the Manchester newspapers were not interested, but, given that the city had a livelier scene in arts and culture than Liverpool, Rose's place within that scene, and the fact that he did most of his best work in Manchester, suggests that he retained a certain nostalgia for Liverpool:

ON REVISITING LIVERPOOL. BY ROBERT ROSE, THE BARD OF COLOUR.

SINCE last I wandered by the Mersey's shore
And heard its undulating billows roar,
As if it seemed instinct with the loud noise
Of mirth, and echoed to my heartfelt joys,
Buoyant as the gay vessels in their pride,
Which bound in triumph o'er its foaming tide,
How friends are dead, or far away!
Such changes happen in life's little day. As on I saunter
    pensively along,
Muttering some charm of memory's mournful song,
I turn back to each busy, crowded street, —
But of once merry friends how few I meet!
Strange faces and new forms I see around, —
The tide of life doth everywhere abound,
And still rolls on, as Mersey's flowing wave,
Heedless of all whose home is now the grave.
T'is saddening still to find how soon forgot

Are those who once with ours did twine their lot;
And yet, if 'twere not so, a settled gloom
Would brood o'er men, prophetic of the tomb.
Far better still should life pursue its way,
In all its triumph, as I've seen to-day:
Though some be sad, let those who can be gay.
'Tis not designed that we should ever mourn
For those, alas! who never can return,
Neglecting duties and the blessings given.
By the All wise to lure our souls to heaven:
As for the absent, soon their vacant place
Is filled by others in life's crowded race,
As gay in hope as they were: but, in turn,
They, too, must yield it up for death's dark bourne,
While friends may come o'er them, like me, to mourn.
Fain would I ask for those I miss,—but dread
To hear the – awful answer, 'They are dead.'
[*Liverpool Albion*, 12 September 1842]

Rose's final address was 10 St Stephen's Street in Salford, although he is not listed as a member of Mrs Fentem's household there in the 1841 census. Sometime shortly after that census, probably in 1842, Rose moved into 10 St Stephen's Street as a lodger. The house would have been quite close to Henry Wilmot Jones's house, where Rose had enjoyed many a convivial evening; although the soirees would have ceased by then as Henry Jones died in 1841 and his housemate, Philip Bailey, had left to return to Nottingham, while John Bolton Rogerson and Rose were by this time heavily involved with the Sun Inn Poets on Long Millgate. It may be that Rose had in fact found his lodgings through his Long Millgate connections. The name of his landlady, Mrs Fentem, is an unusual one, and there is only one Fentem listed in the Manchester Directories of 1840–1. Henry Fentem was a grocer and tea dealer who had premises at 140 Long Millgate and this coincidence is probably not to be ignored. John Bolton Rogerson would doubtless have provided an introduction. The shop was just over a mile from the Fentem house, a brisk fifteen minute walk. Rose was still residing there when he died, so he may have paid a retainer fee if and when he did go travelling.

St Stephen's Street was then a street of typical solid Victorian houses and No. 10 may have been a general lodging house. Across the way from No. 10 stood St Stephen's Church (1794–1956), a low brick building with a central square tower forming the entrance. St Stephen's Tavern stood at 53 St Stephen's Street, just a short distance away, which would have been handy for Rose. Today the houses have long gone and where No. 10 might have stood there is a modern office block which stands alone towards the end of what is now a long wide tree-lined street. Because Mrs Fentem was Rose's landlady at the time of his death, it is from her evidence that much of the sadness of his last years becomes obvious. Downtown Salford might have seemed an unusual choice for Rose to make his home, but in his day St Stephen's Street was a fairly recent modern street on the western edge of Salford, not far from the River Irwell.

Judging from his ongoing relationship with the press, his letters and his poems, it becomes clear that Robert Rose had still not returned to 'the land of his birth' by 1842. A possible reason is that after 1838 his main reason for returning would have been to reunite with his mother, but she may well have died by then since he does not refer to her at all in his later poetry. His other main reason for returning may have been his fascination with the ocean, which he mentions in several of his poems. He had announced his intention of writing a major poetical work about the ocean, but, like many of his other intended works which were advertised with his earlier poems, it would seem that he was not 'a finisher', perhaps distracted by drink or social pleasures. At the end of the pamphlet containing his poem on 'The Coronation' there is a promotional notice for works either lost or never written:

> Shortly will be Published, by ROBERT ROSE, THE ISLES OF INDIA, a Poem. To be followed by The Pleasures of Solitude, a Poem; Recollections of the Departed, being a series of Sonnets; A Vision of Life; Essays on English Oratory; Thoughts on Moral Philosophy; Songs of the Past; Literary Letters; and An Enquiry into the Means of Happiness. LONGMAN and Co. London.

Chapter Eight

'Awake! Inspiring Muse...'

Early in 1838 Rose had written a short poem simply called 'The Bazaar', which was considered a little daring, because although it praised the queen, it also alluded to the French Revolution of 1789 scarcely fifty years beforehand and still within living memory.

The Bazaar
Say! Muse is this a picture of thy land
A vision summoned by a fairy wand?
What objects here unite to charm mankind,
To warm with rapture th' expansive mind,
To lend bright influence to this varied place,
Where circles loveliness in all we trace!
Soft o'er the sense the sound of music steals
And every heart the pleasing influence feels;
Quick quivers through each frame the mellow notes,
While all around in trembling rapture floats
The sweet embodied joy, and the rapt soul
In glad surprise submits to its control.
Though art with nature beauteously combine,
Yet here the British Fair all else outshine,
And give such lustre to this gay Bazaar,
As will, we hope, draw myriads from afar
True as the magnet to the Polar Star.
As Rome's fair virgins watch'd the holy flame.
Thus guards our mental lamps, each gentle dame
Who govern here so mildly and serene,

Each multiplies the image of the Queen!
The glorious days of valiant France were three,*
In which Success shook hands with Liberty

[* alluding to the three days of the French Revolution.]

Considering the fate of the French queen, Marie Antoinette, Rose was perhaps fortunate to get away with the reference, but one of his first major works written in Manchester was to celebrate the coronation of Queen Victoria, although it was mainly Liverpool newspapers who commented upon it in judgement. Rose had had copies bound, together with a lesser piece on Sunday schools, one of which he sent to the queen. The queen let it be known through one of her ladies-in-waiting that she approved of the poem, so he had decided to sell 'The Coronation' in pamphlet form rather than have it printed by the newspapers.

The poem was quite long (around 2,000 words), sometimes rather verbose for modern tastes, and it might have benefited from being broken down into more stanzas. Rose's obsession with rhyming couplets led, on occasion, to some clumsy use of language, but he was sufficiently complimentary and self-effacing to be acceptable to the queen, who, although only 18, had fairly exalted ideas about herself. The poem is too long to reproduce in full here, but excerpts will give some idea of its nature. It was both praised and criticised. Although perhaps not to modern tastes and not carrying the power of more modern free verse, or less inhibited poetry, it should be assessed within the context of its times: it was written nearly 200 years ago by a man from another culture. It impressed Queen Victoria and it enjoyed sales and reprints, all in pamphlet form. While it might be out of place in a twenty-first century 'pints and poets' down at the local pub, 'The Coronation' was, in early Victorian England, generally regarded as an accomplished success. Doubtless the

Liverpool newspapers were miffed at being unable to publish the poem in their pages, as that might affect sales of the poem in pamphlet form and some reviewers were unable to resist a spot of sniping.

The Coronation
Awake! Aspiring muse, indulging one lay
To Britain's Queen on this auspicious day!
Like incense, pour thy humble tribute forth
To her who rules the noblest land on earth.
Th'occasions great, exalt my humble soul
With 'thoughts that breathe' in melody to role;
Pervade my mind til through th'electric frame
There dart a Patriot and a Poet's flame!
Thou who awok'st when ag'd Britannia's King*
Slept 'neath a greater monarch's powerful sting;
Thou who Hast sung of stars and moon of yore,
And bathed in the deep stream of ancient lore,
Awake! and sound the quivering string once more.
Oh, that to me were sent the gifts of song,
To rush in rapture like a tide along;
Then I would raise a glorious strain, I ween,
Fit for the ears of England's peerless Queen!
Then would such strain repay me with delight
For the bold wish to climb the Parnassian height,
But vain this wish, for I have not the power;
I, puny minstrel of the passing hour,
Fearing to step before the public gaze,
To dare its censure or to court its praise,
Living my brief space, to be heard no more,
Must sink to rest with millions gone before.
Yes! I am doom'd from earth to pass away,
The short-lived insect of one little day;

Therefore, I call on one who can inspire
The world – to rise! – too long hath slept his lyre!
**Southey, thou prince of the living Bards, arise!
And let thy glad notes echo to the skies;
Thou Priest of Nature, great! whose hallow'd shrine
Emits indulgence which is part divine,
'Tis thine to thrill the soul, while dwells with thee
The virtuous influence of Poesy!
Strike once again thy slumbering golden string,
Tune it to her to whom all Bards should sing;
For I am one quite humble in the crowd,
Soon to be wrapped in cold oblivion's shroud;
But thy fame will roll down the stream of ages
Among th'immortal band of Bards and Sages –

[*   Refers to the death of Victoria's uncle, William IV, in June 1837.

** Rose greatly admired Robert Southey who was the English Poet
    Laureate from 1813 until his death in 1843.]

Southey belonged to the Romantic poets, like his great friend, Samuel Coleridge, but he was criticised in later life for becoming much more establishment, conservative and traditional in his outlook.

Rose knew it was a great honour to write the poem and to have the queen's approval but at the same time it must have secretly jarred with his inner being and his conviction that all people were, or should be, equal. He was painfully aware of the real situation and must have inwardly cringed at some of what he clearly felt impelled to write:

But if to elevate the human race,
By shedding on them thy celestial grace,
To balance justice with an equal hand,
Until thy name be praised in every land;
Until the god of Mercy smile on thee,

And sanctify each kind, yet just decree;
Until thy virtues through all time resound,
And waft thy power to earth's remotest bound;
If to do this, and rule with gentle sway,
While millions bask beneath the genial ray,
And be like Summer chasing Winter now,
Then blest art thou with honours on thy brow!
Stronger are thine than claims of warrior's glory,
To be remembered in all future story;
Then shall thy greatest strength, or bliss alone,
Be a warm people's love around thy Throne.

The lines 'If to do this, and rule with gentle sway, While millions bask beneath the genial ray,' were written while his countrymen were still bound by slavery 'apprenticeships' (i.e. further years of slavery); and the millscapes consumed people's lives with seventy-hour weeks for minimal wages meaning that most lived in squalor and deprivation and died young. Few 'basked beneath the genial ray'.

Slavery, discrimination, complete dismissal of those not who were not white, had kept Rose from his homeland and searching for his obviously adored mother; and the rigid 'class system', which still affects England in the twenty-first century, meant only a very comparative few had the time and means 'to bask in genial rays'. The reviews were generally all favourable but he had hit on a winning formula of praising a popular new young queen with the inevitable patriotic fervour of the time, even if it was rather forced for him personally. He knew the score well enough, and he managed to bury his resentment, even though he must have silently prayed for forgiveness for what he would have seen as the obsequiousness of some of his words.

THE CORONATION: a Poem. With Reflections on the occasion. Dedicated to Her Most Gracious Majesty Queen Victoria. To which is annexed, a POEM ON

SUNDAY SCHOOLS. By ROBERT ROSE, a West Indian of Colour. FOURTH EDITION, With Opinions on the Press. Mr R. Rose, the well-known 'poet of colour', has written some pleasing lines on the all-engrossing theme, the coronation of our beautiful Queen. As a loyal subject, and an ardent admirer, his strain is at once addressed for her happiness as a woman and a Queen; nor does his muse forget that much of that happiness will depend upon her efforts to promote the well-being, comfort, and prosperity of her subjects.

[*Manchester and Salford Advertiser*]

This is a poem by Mr Robert Rose, a West Indian, several of whose productions formerly appeared in our columns. Notwithstanding the hasty, manner in which it is written, our readers will find in it much to commend, &c.

[*Liverpool Albion*, 9 July 1838]

We noticed this little poem in the coronation week—while yet in manuscript. It is now published, and will well reward a careful perusal. The subject is one of universal interest, the coronation of our youthful and beloved Queen. Mr ROSE, although a West Indian, is an Englishman in sentiment and loyal devotion, and evidently overflowing with the most chivalrous respect to the women.

[*Manchester and Salford Advertiser*, 14 July 1838]

Mr Rose, the author of this poem, is well known in Liverpool as the writer of several other productions, which are highly creditable to his feelings and his attainments. The versification in this poem is smooth and correct: the language and imagery are chaste and beautiful. We need scarcely add that the sentiments breathed throughout are devotedly loyal.

[*Liverpool Standard* 17 July 1838]

As Mr Rose is very well known in Liverpool, we copy the subjoined notice of one of his most recent productions from a contemporary: — 'It is seldom that we can spare much room to dwell on poetry, but when we observe a poem by an old correspondent, loyally dedicated to her most gracious majesty, which production evinces talent of no common order, we are tempted to recommend it to the notice of our enlightened readers. Mr Rose, as they are well aware, is a West Indian, and is remarkable for blending philosophic truth with the blandishments of poetry. He is happy in his choice of words and melodious in his versification. We look upon the earnest manner in which he writes as a good presage of future success.'

[*Liverpool Mercury*, 20 July 1838]

'The Coronation.' A clever little poem, bearing this title, has just been forwarded to us. The author is Mr Robert Rose, a West Indian of colour, well known as the author of several beautiful pieces of poetry, some of which we have had the pleasure to copy into this paper. The present production is highly creditable to the author, and contains some very sweet poetry, and not less captivating sentiment. We are glad to learn that the poetic efforts of this interesting (interesting on many accounts) writer have met with a gratifying share of public appreciation.

[*Preston Chronicle*, 21 July 1838]

We have given above, in this column, an extract from the poem which Mr Rose has recently published on that previously threadbare subject—the coronation of Queen Victoria. The production of Mr Rose displays no inconsiderable share of Poetic beauty, and will, we trust, have an extensive set. The author is already favourably known in Liverpool by his contributions to the press of the town.

[*Liverpool Chronicle*, 21 July 1838]

A poem under this title, by Robert Rose, a West Indian of colour, has been submitted to us. It evinces a degree of talent highly creditable to the author and is accompanied by a poem on Sunday Schools not less worthy of favourable notice.

[*Bell's Life*, 29 July 1838]

These are endurable lines, &c.

[*Sunday Times*, 29 July 1838]

In submitting the remarks of the press to the reader according to their dates, the Author is happy to state that not one unfavourable critique of the foregoing Poems has appeared. This he is the more proud of, as it is somewhat rare for anyone, in these days of smart competition, to meet with the approval of the (generally speaking) conflicting opinions of the press. He would gladly have waited for other important notices but can delay no longer in bringing out this edition. Shortly will be Published, by ROBERT ROSE, THE ISLES OF INDIA, a Poem. To be followed by The Pleasures of Solitude, a Poem; Recollections of the Departed, being a series of Sonnets; A Vision of Life; Essays on English Oratory; Thoughts on Moral Philosophy; Songs of the Past; Literary Letters; and An Enquiry into the

Means of Happiness. LONGMAN and Co. London; ADVERTISER OFFICE, WHEELER, ELLERBY, LEWIS, Manchester; E. SMITH and Co., ARNOLD, Liverpool; and all other Booksellers. Price One Shilling.

[*Liverpool Standard* 19 October 1838]

Mr Robert Rose's Coronation Poem- We COPY the following notice of Mr – Rose's work from the Monthly Magazine: - The Coronation; a Poem. By Robert Rose, West Indian of colour. Second edition. Longman and Co.- This poem contains some very pretty images and sentiments which all breathe a spirit of loyalty and respect towards the fair subject of the lay. The following verses are thought by the author to be not inapplicable to her gracious Majesty, whom he has never seen, but by imagination. We cannot say that we admire this idle and fulsome compliment. We, however, transcribe the lines alluded to for their own poetic merits. Here follows a tolerably long extract from the poem, which our other arrangements oblige us to omit, referring our readers to the work itself Edit. Mer.

[*Liverpool Mercury*, Friday, 28 September 1838]

However, Rose had clearly prevented the *Liverpool Mercury* from publishing extracts because the poem was being published in pamphlet form, and he was obviously not keen for newspapers to publish anything which might detract from sales. It is hard not to wonder, though, if the *Liverpool Mercury* later got their own back on Rose. Despite the early good reviews Robert Rose never took criticism of his poetry easily:

MR ROSE, THE BARD OF COLOUR. TO THE EDITOR OF THE ALBION. SIR,—The February number of the Wesleyan Association Magazine having been shown to me, I find, to my surprise, my ' Coronation

Poem' criticised under the name of Robert Bruce, a West Indian, instead of Robert Rose. Now, glad as I should be for any native of the West Indies to come forward as a votary of the muse, or in an any other capacity as an author striving to advance in the progression of intellectual improvement, yet I believe, (and it is a matter more of regret than exultation to me,) that, however mean my abilities are, I stand in the peculiarly isolated position of being the first and only one in the field. How such a mistake could have been made, without it has been either waggishly or spitefully perpetrated, is to me inexplicable. As the circumstance might do a slight injury, which ought never to be suffered with impunity, I resolved it should not be passed over in silence.

Yours, respectfully, ROBERT ROSE.
[*Liverpool Albion*, Monday, 25 March 1839]

Later that week the *Liverpool Mercury* received and published a very similar letter:

MR ROSE, THE BARD OF COLOUR. – To the EDITOR of the LIVERPOOL MERCURY

Sir,-The February number of the *Wesleyan Association Magazine* having been shown to me, I find, to my extreme surprise; my 'Coronation Poem' criticised under the name of 'Robert Bruce, a West Indian,' instead of Robert Rose. Now, glad as I should be for any native of the West Indies to come forward as a votary of the Muse, or in any other capacity as an author, yet I believe I am at present time the first and only one in the field; and therefore, how such a mistake could have been made, without it, has been waggishly or spitefully perpetrated is to me inexplicable As the circumstance might do me a slight injury, I resolved it should not be passed over in silence.

Yours etc. ROBERT ROSE.

[*Liverpool Mercury*, Friday, 29 March 1839]

It could simply have been a mischievous referral to Rose's supposed origins since Robert Bruce was a medieval king of Scotland, and Robert Rose was a Black king of poetry whose father was considered to be very possibly Scottish. The *Mercury*, however, decided to make light of it, and, in modern terms, used the 'glitch in the system' explanation:

> One of our printers' imps, who is a most outrageous and incorrigible punster, suggests that the above communication should be prefaced with the motto,-
>
> 'That which we call a Rose by any other name would smell as sweet.' Edit.Merc

Chapter Nine

'I feel a chilling weight press on my heart...'

Rose liked company, and he was both sociable and hospitable, but he seemed to actively seek out white companions, rather than those of his own ethnic background. He may have met other Black writers and abolitionists, but there is no record that he did so, and it is almost certain that there would have been comments. Perhaps memories would have been evoked that were too painful. Rose appears to shy away from emotion in person, although he does try to express emotion through his poetry. It was clear from a poem written early in 1838 to a girl he was leaving behind (who he does not name) that he was still intending to return to his homeland:

A melancholy comes on me
Whene'er we meet !—
'tis not that beauty bright
I disavow, though soon, alas! it flee,
Not that I may not bask beneath thy light
And thrill before thy presence; but I feel
A chilling weight press on my heart, to think
The influence of years will on thee steal
And sever, one by one, thy beauty's link.
Soon the vast world of ocean will bear me
To Indian climes; but, ere departing hence,
By all the hours spent here so happily,
I would, kind Fate, thy virtues recompense:

To Heaven I pour my warm devotions forth,
That thine may be a happy lot on earth.
                    [*Liverpool Albion*, 13 March 1838]

It was a well-known fact that Rose like to parade in the town with a girl or two on his arm. There is a brief mention of him visiting Chetham's Library in jovial mood with a girl on each arm. He also frequented the Portico Library, although there are no accounts of him visiting the Portico while escorting young ladies. There are, of course, no clues as to who these girls were, but it was clear he enjoyed their company. It is tempting to wonder if the girl who was the subject of a poem in June 1839 was the same girl to whom he was bidding farewell in March 1838. He had not yet set sail for 'Indian climes' and he was clearly mourning someone who recently died. As in the 'Cypress Wreath' Rose does his mourning at one remove. He does not indicate if the lost friend in 'Departed' was male or female, but his use of language suggests female. 'The lov'd companion of each tranquil scene … To wander musing through some whisp'ring grove, Or watch the vesper star serenely shine…'

THE DEPARTED. BY ROBERT ROSE, THE BARD OF COLOUR.

Oh friend! for ever lov'd, not ever lost,
While I remain on life's rough ocean tost,
My fancy paints thee still as thou hast been,
The lov'd companion of each tranquil scene;
How wert thou wont to scorn the giddy race
Who flutter still in ardent pleasure's chase,
Who, 'neath unalter'd fate,—man's common doom,
Still fall unmourn'd, unhonour'd to the tomb;
But thou did'st prize the Poet's art, and love
To wander musing through some whisp'ring grove,
Or watch the vesper star serenely shine,
Anticipating 'thence that land divine

Whence thou art gone, for whom we shed the tear,
Though thou perchance art happy in its sphere.
[*Liverpool Albion*, 10 June 1839]

By the end of the 1830s the character of Robert Rose was starting to become rather morbid and gloomy. One of his favourite forms of poetry was the sonnet; although he was keen on stanzas, more often than not he wrote in rhyming couplets, which could be limiting and sometimes he struggled with them. Frequently, his themes seemed to be separation or death and the grave.

BY THE BARD OF COLOUR.
When I reflect on the gloomy grave,
Where still sink the beauteous and the brave—
How it closes o'er our fairest schemes,
And disperses our most dazzling dreams;
And hath no respect for youth or age,
But with all a dreadful war loth wage;—
When I reflect on this transient earth,
With all its woe aid its empty mirth,
How frail man still is born to sorrow,
Now here to-day, and gone to-morrow;
And how rolling generations pass
Like the phantom forms of Banquo's glass;
I confess the tear bedews my eye,
As I muse on man's sad destiny.
But when I think of Heaven, where care
Nor grief shall taint its fragrant air,
I glory in this brief mortal space,
That this world's not our abiding place;
The less here of earth, the more there of love,
In the halcyon homes of the climes above!
[*Liverpool Standard* 7 December 1838]

Four months later he is lamenting yet another death of a lady he had failed to visit in time, and in this case some of the rhyming couplets are strained:

HAPPY END. BY ROBERT ROSE, THE BARD OF COLOUR.

Sinks to the grave with imperceiv'd decay,
While resignation gently slopes the way;
And all her prospects brightening to the last,
Her heaven commences ere the world be past.
How could I bear her end was near
Without emotions deep and drear?
A shock, convulsing all my frame,
Burst on me; she, whose gentle name,
With magic soft, could guide the stream
Of feeling; she who seemed a dream
All bright, or vestal flame watch'd by
The friends who linger'd ever nigh
Where'er her steps inclined to roam, —
Must she then quit her earthly home?
That holy beam extinguished quite,
Which flicker'd in transcendent light,
And shone, in gracious majesty,
Within a peerless canopy,
Inviting all wound to move
Within the silken bonds of love.
She, whose fair mind, like zephyr calm,
Diffus'd full wide its genial balm—
Beneficently shedding round
Its halo pure with virtue crown'd.

The shades of death I might not see
Lowering upon her destiny;

I was too late to bid farewell
To her whose spirit was a spell
To make of earth a lowly heaven,
To faith and virtue ever given.
But what broke gently on my pain?
'Twas hope that breathed
'We'll meet again!'
Like a soft whispering seraph there
She banish'd frenzy and despair.
What, though her friends, with features pale,
Rais'd round her couch the pitying wail,
She, she alone smil'd satisfied,
Compos'd her quiv'ring limbs, and died.

Yes, I was late, life's spark was past,
Too pure for earth, she could not last;
Before her end a radiance played
O'er the blanch'd cheek, so soon to fade
In death ,—'twas a calm evening light
Compared to that Cimmesian night
Which shrouds o'er those who walk the road
Of sin, to face an angry God!
Her soul receiv'd the hand divine,
And bow'd before the heavenly shrine;
And then, as pure as angel-thought,
Its last long home confiding sought:
And, as at sweet decline of day,
The sun glides peacefully away;
So, when the Almighty made her blest,
Her saintly spirit fled to rest.

[Liverpool Albion, 15 April 1839]

Chapter Ten

'All are not men who bear the name...'

'To A Man', (from the weekly dispatch, the original of which is held by Chetham's) is a sonnet written by Rose during the period of his disagreement with the *Liverpool Mercury*. He renamed his sonnet before publication in the *Dublin Herald* as 'All are not men who bear the name', in which he establishes the characteristics of what he feels constitutes 'a real man':

If thou art rich, let all thy kindness share;
If thou art poor, learn poverty hear;
If high and mighty, tread not on the low,
A very worm may turn a serpent foe;
In every station act in such way
As will give comfort at some future day.
If young, repress the warmth of passion's rage,
So that thou call not down reproof from age,
If old still look with tenderness on youth
Let thy experience be their guide to truth:
Let youth and age still journey, hand in hand
Together, searching for better land.
Thus, onward move, and through life's little span,
Thus prove thy highest claim to a man.
ROBERT ROSE, the Bard of Colour.

[*Dublin Weekly Herald*, 2 March 1839]

'The Coronation' had enhanced Rose's reputation as a poet of note and his fame was spreading. Poetically, if not personally, speaking, Robert Rose was on a roll, and he had printed another poem in pamphlet form in 1839:

> 'The Bazaar, a Poem; embracing thoughts on the progressive knowledge in connection with it.' Robert Rose, the Bard of Colour. Manchester: Belshaw. This poem was composed by desire of the friends of the Manchester Mechanics' Institution, to whom it is inscribed. The occasion which gave rise to it was the Bazaar recently held at Manchester, for the benefit of the Mechanics' Institution. The versification is smooth, and the sentiments correct. We are glad to find that Mr Rose's talents are held in such high estimation by our Manchester neighbours.
>
> [*Liverpool Standard* 11 October 1839]

Rose seemed to have gone silent on the questions of discrimination, slavery, equality, and the concept that all people are people under the skin, about which he had been so passionate in his 1835 speech, but he was supporting and promoting education because he saw education as means to achieve equality and a better life while defeating ignorance and its resulting discriminations. By the end of 1839, capitalising on his poetical talents, he was giving lectures on poetry to Manchester audiences as noted by a report in the *Leeds Times*:

> Robert Rose, a negro* bard, has been delivering lectures on poetry at the Manchester Parthenon [now the Manchester Art Gallery on Mosley Street].
>
> [*Leeds Times*, Saturday, 28 December 1839]

[* The use of the word 'negro' (the Spanish word for black) is considered offensive today and Robert Rose may also have thought the same way because it was around this time that he began to style himself 'the Bard of Colour'.]

THE FESTIVAL OF KNOWLEDGE

LIFT up your hopes, ye friends of knowledge, free
Swell high the accordant shout of social glee!
And let the fretted domes re-echo round!
For, from this spot, I trust, a glorious sound
Will hence flow forth to speak the might of mind,
Strong as the rolling wave or rushing wind.
Bright as the lightning on its fiery wing,
And lovely as the sweet return of spring,
Such this inspiring night! fair pledge of hope,
That to our vision give unbounded scope
Of the great mental work so begun,
That tells, by banners glittering in the sun,
Knowledge shall yet progress from clime to clime,
And win the clarion praises of all time.

Note.—The above is in commemoration of a complimentary supper given to the author, by his friends in Manchester, which, in every respect, was an educational gathering,
ROBERT ROSE, THE BARD OF COLOUR.
[*Liverpool Albion*, Monday, 3 August 1840]

Mechanics' Exhibition.—The mechanics' exhibition which has been productive of such good results to the institution on Cooper-street, closed on Monday, the 29 ult., after the promenade which had been announced for the evening, M. Bally took cast from a living subject. The vocal music, and the beautiful experiment of the fire cloud, by Mr Day, which was made more interesting than usual, then followed; after which, the assembly adjourned to the picture gallery, where Mr Robert Rose, the bard of colour, proposed a vote of thanks to the committee who had superintended the exhibition, to all those who had contributed in any way to its valuable object, and to the ladies for their attendance, which were passed with three hearty cheers; the assembly then separated. The nett receipts of the exhibition are not yet exactly computed, but are supposed to be about four hundred pounds [over £21,000 today]. Correspondent.

[*Manchester Courier and Lancashire General Advertiser*, Saturday, 4 July 1840]

MANCHESTER MECHANICS' INSTITUTION.-A coffee afternoon consisting of ladies and gentlemen, was held at the Mechanics' Institution on Thursday, on the occasion of opening the discussion class for the season; Mr Benjamin Fothergill in the chair. Mr Robert Rose, the bard of colour, who had been fixed upon to commence the proceedings for the season, read an elaborate paper on the present state of education, which was well received, and formed the theme for the evening's amusement, parties making remarks thereon, by which visitors were able to form an idea how the gratifying proceedings are carried on in general on other nights when the society is not opened to the public as it was on this occasion.

[*Manchester Times*, Saturday, 5 September 1840]

Rose was probably now at the zenith of his literary career. His speech on abolition and emancipation had been published and sold well, and so too had his poem on the coronation of Queen Victoria. He had been accepted by the Sun Inn Poets on Long Millgate and was now their vice chairman. He gave lectures on poetry (but not on slavery, abolition, emancipation or equality) which appear to have been well received, and his general output began to increase; although an appreciation of his poetry was not always forthcoming.

However, by the early 1840s his mood was growing ever darker and he expressed his feelings though his poetry but his continuing insistence on the forms of sonnets or rhyming couplets sometimes made his language clumsy as he tried to fit his emotions into rhyme. The poem for which mixed reviews began to appear is reproduced here courtesy of the *Liverpool Albion* who printed it in the early autumn of 1840. Modern readers may agree with the *Northern Star*'s dismissal of the work, but it has to be seen in the context of the times in which it was written. In the twenty-first century death is often seen as a taboo subject, but in the nineteenth century it was so much a part of daily life that poems like the 'Cypress Wreath' would be seen as a fitting comment rather than as an endless dirge. While it is true that Robert Rose was not among the most well known or memorable poets of his time – he was not a Keats or a Byron or a Shelley – he was generally judged to be competent. His poem might have been much more powerful if he had stayed with the unfortunate young lady until she died instead of running away yet again from a deathbed at a time when he should have been putting her first and not himself. It almost makes his poetic interpretation of her death rather more impersonal because he simply did not witness it himself:

**Cypress Wreath: The Bard's Cypress Wreath or
Elegy on the Death of a Young Lady**

**Inscribed to her bereaved parents, Mr &
Mrs Fothergill**

By Robert Rose, The Bard of Colour
A breathing pause is ours to think at last
Now grief's tremendous thunder-shock is past:

But, after all, 'twas only death who came;
His brow of terror and his dart of flame, scathed not th'
   immortal and enfranchised mind
That upward soar'd and left the earth far behind;
She that was here, a fleeting bird of love,
Is now an angel at the throne above.
'Tis a blest change to a far happier state,
Howe'er inflicting was the rod of fate;
And, after all, what was it but a groan?
A tear, a sad farewell! And she was gone
To bloom through heaven's long amaranthine year:
Then, why for this, should flow the unmanly tear?
We're racers after death, e'en from our birth,
Each day prepares to lay us in the earth.

Green be the grass that grows upon her grave;
Calm be her sleep where the dark yew-trees wave;
Let no unhallow'd step disturb the ground,
May spirits of the good there hover round
To guard the sacred place, and we will strew
The earliest flowers spring spreads unto our view,
Emblems of her pass'd in her primrose spring,
And let the night-bird there all sorrowing sing.

While we will wander oft at silent eve
'Neath the bright stars beside her tomb to grieve:
And when through the tall trees the low winds creep,
We'll think her voice breaths softly, 'Do not weep!'
'Tis for ourselves that we should mourn the most,
And not for her, but for a brief while lost;
Heaven hath now claim'd her, God calls first on those
He loves the most, from this world and its woes.

The less of this dim earth, the more of heaven,
This consolation still to us is given;
Death was her kindest friend, he gave release
From earth to happiness and endless peace!
Parents and kindred mourn not! but on high
See how the queen of the night from the vast sky
Seems beckoning to you, with a look all holy,
As if it long'd to soothe your melancholy.

Was it not wisely ordered she fled young?
Why mourn, then, like a lyre that's all unstrung?
How many are there 'neath the trackless wave,
Of whom grief cannot point the watery grave?
Yours is a happier lot! you have a sign
Exalting the terrestrial to divine;
Pointing to heaven from earth she hath a tomb,
Type of the past, grave-record of her doom.

How many are there sink without a friend
To smooth their pillow, and there fondly tend?
But had she not a mother's tender aid,
And, father, brother, sisters round her bed?
To rob the serpent death of his foul sting,
And bless her on her heavenward journeying
On to her Eden home, where angels throng,
To hail the new arrival with sweet song.

I did not see her end, I could not view
A woman die, and one who loved so true.
To think that she, on whom life open'd fair,
Is shut from the glad sunshine and free air,
And this bright world, would stultify each sense,

Did not the justice of Omnipotence
Proclaim in characters by truth unfurled
'There is another and a better world!'*

[* The last part of this powerful conclusion becomes more striking
as a climax, from the mournfully thrilling interest attached to the
circumstance of poor Palmer, the actor, who, it is said, was struck
dead while repeating the impressive words of this passage, or
shortly after, at the Liverpool Theatre.]

[*Liverpool Albion*, 28 September 1840]

NOTICES OF NEW PUBLICATIONS. THE BARD'S CYPRESS WREATH; ON THE DEATH OF A YOUNG LADY: INSCRIBED TO THE BEREAVED PARENTS. BY ROBERT ROSE, THE BARD OF COLOUR, AND LAUREATE OF THE WESTERN ISLES.

Mr Robert Rose has, certainly, a most prolific pen, and we are bound in fairness to admit, that his industry is highly commendable. We should be better pleased, however, with his multitudinous compositions if, in presenting such an abundance of words, he gave us 'more matter' with more art. At present he gives us 'words, words, words', sometimes strung into tolerable rhymes, and, occasionally, perfect in metre, but lacking several other qualities which the world has agreed in considering essential to true poetry. The writer who mistakes extravagant notions, dressed in high-flown language, for indications of imaginative power, and who deals in trifling conceits and false metaphors, presuming all the time that he is exhibiting a glowing fancy, may succeed in pleasing himself, and, mayhap, a few partial friends, but the favourable regard of the public will be in the inverse ratio of the frequency with which he appears before them. With these opinions we would advise Mr Rose to hang up his lute for a time, or, at least, to practise on it in private till he has acquired a more masterly touch. He has, from time to time, sent us many pieces, which we have inserted at his request, more from a desire that the public should have a fair opportunity of judging of his powers than from any opinion which we entertained of their superior merit as compositions. It seems to us that he writes too much to write well, and that he regards quantity more than quality. If the *cacoethes scribendi* be so strong upon him that he cannot resist its impulse, let him write! but it would be well if he would then lay his pieces aside till the ardour which prompted him has subsided. If he will read them during a cool interval, he will, probably, be enabled to give them considerable improvement.

[*Liverpool Albion*, 28 September 1840]

THE BARD'S CYPRESS WREATH; on the Death of a Young Lady-Inscribed to her Be-reaved Parents. By ROBERT Rose, the Bard of Colour, and Laureate of the Western Isles. London: Henry Johnson, 49, Paternoster-row; Manchester, Bancks and Co.; Liverpool, Davies and Co. From announcements adroitly posted at the beginning and end of the book, we learn that this is intended by the author as a feeler. We learn that the public are to be laid under further obligation to the 'Laureate of the Western Isles'; but we much fear whether the acknowledgement will at all accord with the expectancies of the 'Bard of Colour'; at least, if his promised pieces be upon a par in point of merit with the one before us. The best thing we find in it is in the preface:- 'The author regrets that he has not talent sufficient to give permanency to his subject.' We feel compelled to subscribe most cordially to the author's criticism of his own work.

[*Northern Star and Leeds General Advertiser,*
3 October 1840]

The *Northern Star* is rather more blunt, although the *Liverpool Albion* critique hints that the newspaper is beginning to find Rose rather tiresome but, nevertheless, the paper continued to print his poems. Robert Rose would continue to find fault, but he tried to shrug off these criticisms and wrote what he considered a merry little poem for Christmas 1840 which was published by the *Manchester Times*:

CHRISTMAS. By ROBERT ROSE, the Bard of Colour, and Laureate of the West Indies.

Old Christmas once more visits us with frozen mien of
    grace,
His steps through country and through town, how
    cheerily we trace:
What feelings now of festive glee are bounding in the
    heart,
Feelings that from life's earliest dawn can never all
    depart.
Mankind at merry Christmas time fling sorrow to the
    wind,
And rich, and poor, and old, and young, are then all free
    and kind;
The general pulse of joy beats high, there is no throb of
    sorrow,
Let cups then circle sparkingly,
Mirth cares not for the morrow!

Old Christmas blythe and hearty comes, as he was wont
  of yore,
Like hunter with his bugle-hour, to sound at each man's
  door:
And though his ancient sports are gone, still can he grief
  beguile,
Glad poor men's hearts, make young the old, and bid the
  rich to smile.
Old Christmas shakes his hoary head, with fun and
  fancy free,
And cries aloud to every man, 'I must see gaiety';
Away! with melancholy thoughts, my reign is now
  begun,
You've time enough to dwell on these when I again am
  gone.
'Hark! hark a lively stir awakes, and throbs throughout
  the hall-
Tis jolly Christmas entering free and shaking hands
  with all;
As needle to the magnet speeds, warm hearts in concord
  meet,
And friendship, mirth, and music join e'en envious time
  to cheat.
Huzzah! we herald Christmas in with laughter, love, and
  song,
And may thy sprightly fingers, Joy! the fairy strains
  prolong,
Such as the minstrel fain would seek, who terminates
  this rhyme,
By wishing all men bounteous cheer at merry Christmas-
  time.

    [*Manchester Times*, Saturday, 26 December 1840]

Chapter Eleven

'May knowledge spread from pole to pole...'

Robert Rose was very keen on universal education which he felt was the way to a better life and a better world. He had long championed Mechanics' Institutes which allowed people academic learning or practical training through evening classes after their day's work was done. Rose had had a good education himself and he believed that education would help to solve many social problems, especially that of crime. He wrote a poem about education and crime that also clearly demonstrated his distaste for capital punishment which was often meted out for even comparatively minor offences such as stealing a sheep:

The Felon or The Necessity of Universal Education.
By Robert Rose, the Bard of Colour, and Laureate of
the Western Isles.
The judge has left the court to dine.
The lawyers go to quaff their wine,
The crowds haste carelessly away,
Alas! such scenes they see every day;
And not a man shows a sign of sorrow
That a felon must depart tomorrow.
But there is one poor, pining creature,
With grief spread over every feature,
Who stands in tribulation there,
The ghastly image of despair;

It is! Oh! it can be no other
Than the doomed felon's mournful mother,

And there's another by her side,
The maid who was to have been his bride;
Alas! how changed for this sad scene
Their moonlight walks and meadows green.
Oh heavy day! They blend alone
Their tears, when the cold crowds are gone.

Would not such woeful scenes be spared,
If all an education shared?
Pure as the light comes, heaven free,
Strong as the mighty, rolling sea,
Let knowledge speed with giant-tread,
And bruise of crime the serpent head.

While all the nations shall rejoice
To hear the truth the inspiring voice.
Laughing to scorn, mean-born control,
May knowledge spread from pole to pole
Til all men shall united be
In friendship, truth, and unity.

[*Liverpool Albion*, Monday, 22 March 1841]

Rose was, however, becoming rather tetchy and intolerant of mistakes or criticisms. He was by now in his mid-thirties and had achieved neither of his major ambitions of returning to his homeland, nor of writing an epic poem about the ocean.

MR ROSE, THE BARD OF COLOUR, AND THE PRINTERS' IMPS. TO THE EDITOR OF THE ALBION. I observed with pleasure my lines entitled

'The Felon' in your interesting paper. The talented K.H., I remember, used to lash at your printers, sometimes in a humorous way, for their mistakes. I have now to notice one, the first, I must confess, which I have yet discovered in all the numerous pieces which I have had published in your interesting journal; and I should be obliged by your setting it right, either by a remark, or the insertion of this letter. I should not have written to you on the subject, but, as the last lines of the piece stand thus, 'While all men shall unit'd be In Friendship, Truth, and Unity,' the tautology of all met; being united in unity. I need not say, was wrong. It should have been, 'In Friendship, Truth, and Charity.' The mistake almost deserves my inflicting another poetic piece upon you; however, not having time, I spare your columns for the present. While on this subject, I cannot but call to mind a printer's mistake, as humorous as any which has taken place in my whole experience with the press. It was about making its appearance on slips, if I had not luckily called in time at the place where it was being published and corrected it. As the relation of it may be amusing, I quote the lines in which it occurred: 'Though lightnings flash, and storms may loudly rave, On Zion-heights is fixed the good man's set; His hopes expand, far, far beyond the grave: Fierce waves roll impotently at his feet.' Judge of the shock to my nerves when I perused the splendid nonsense the printers had made of it, whist' was thus: 'Fierce waves roll impudently at his feet.' I term it splendid, for had they filed, there would really have been cleverness in making such nonsense out of the difference of only two letters from the word. Sheridan, by only two letters, proved his wit, when he was reported to have praised Gibbon as a luminous historian, he answered, 'I said voluminous': but these printers' imps, in their comical combination of words, would almost make the spirit of Sheridan rise up to laugh at them. Yours, respectfully, ROBERT ROSE. Manchester, 24 March, 1841

[*Liverpool Albion*, 29 March 1841]

THE BARD of COLOUR and the STANDARD, TO THE EDITOR OF THE LIVERPOOL STANDARD. Sir,—As my time, during my short stay in Liverpool, was valuable, I should not have given myself the trouble of calling on you personally, except out of respect to the author of 'A Voice from the Town.' He did not present his poem to you, but gave me copies to distribute as I liked. I selected your paper among others, and therefore considered myself justified in writing what I did, as you would never, but for me, have had the work presented to you. The responsibility rested with myself of laying it out with the press, which responsibility is at all times unpleasant, especially in your case, as it has proved. However, as you have taken a different view, I took the opportunity, previous to my leaving town, of sending you a volume unmarked, in place of the other, as I do not wish you to have my autograph, which your vanity would infer. I now take leave of you with merely stating, so far as my own impression goes, that it is unworthy of an editor, provided he possess gentlemanly feelings or good taste, to bring before the public what is scarcely worthy of private notice. If you were short of matter to fill up paper, you should have extracted from the book sent, and not have put forth such trash as you did.

I feel almost ashamed to take up the pen to reply to it; but, having said this with the utmost good feeling I am willing to make every allowance for your apparent ignorance of the amenities of life, too often owing to a deficiency in a polite education: or to a want of having mixed in good society, which, in justice, I must own, has not been your fault but your misfortune.—Yours, ROBERT ROSE. Manchester, 10 June, 1842.

[*Liverpool Albion*, 13 June 1842]

TO THE EDITOR OF THE STANDARD. '*Genus irritabile*' is the epithet applied to the whole tribe of poets, and, aware of this, it was an act of much imprudence certainly to stir up R. Rose, Esquire, for, strange to say, the smaller the poet, the more intense the irritability! I have only to warn you he is in a most immense and towering passion! and, instead of the 'bard of colour', may now more properly be called the 'bard of choler', at least as regards you! I send this by way of *caveto*, and recommend a sharp look out, as I suppose you would not wish the infliction of a horsewhip from that most tuneful and harmonious swain. Should he foolishly have recourse to this mode of venting his fury, you have your remedy by getting him into a cage if you can; such a fine blackbird will sing as well there as at large.

Poets of all hues have we seen,
A black one only lacking,
Who now a lustre sheds I weep,
Like Day and Martin's blacking!
White mice, white foxes, and white crows
All curious are and rare,

But a black poet and black rose
Must make the nations stare!!
The ladies call him quite 'a love',
Who'll sing and never tire.
A perfect blackbird of the grove
Is Robert Rose, Esquire.
CYGNUS NIGER.

We really have to offer our readers some apology for obtruding before their notice a silly communication from that very silly and vain person, Robert Rose, Esq. (the bard of colour); but as our contemporary, the Albion, in the absence of his usual rubbish, has found room for Robert Rose, Esq. (the bard of colour), we feel bound to admit that we intended giving the letter in our last, and it was actually in type, but thrown out by important matter. As Robert Rose, Esq. (the bard of colour), as it will be seen in the Albion, has omitted the graceful and elegant postscript of his letter, we have no objection to give it, because as we enjoy a good laugh, we fancy our readers participate in the same sort of jokery. We said his letter was funny; and we appeal to anybody if we did not say rightly. All this is, however, wide of the question. Robert Rose, Esq., tries to get a notice of himself, by his friend Rogerson's laudatory poetry, in the STANDARD. We do not choose to be dictated to, 'so we show him up', as Mr Smalt said of Mr Tims. Robert Rose, Esq. (the bard of colour), now takes up a great deal of space in our paper, and we hope he is satisfied. Anything further must really be paid for as an advertisement.

[*Liverpool Standard*...14 June 1842]

ADMITTANCE, ONE SHILLING TO CORRESPONDENTS THE BARD OF COLOUR

AGAIN we received a letter from this poetical personage who is really much sillier than we took him to be. We cannot, in mercy and mercy to our reader's sides, to the reputation of Robert Rose, insert the letter itself. The sub'stance, however,—(as our correspondent has got into his head the absurd notion that the public is very anxious as to his whereabouts)—we are willing to give. Know all men, therefore,—and ladies too, —that Robert Rose, Esq., the bard of colour, 'has during the last three weeks been in Buxton, Fleetwood, Southport, Blackpool & c., enjoying himself in the luxury of bathing!' or, to speak poetically,

'The Rose has been washed, just washed in a shower' of salt and other waters at these various watering places.— We publish this explanation the more readily, as some of our lion hunters, we understand, have imagined that a certain unknown coloured gentlemen, who has lately amused the passengers in one of the Egremont ferry boats, by his exquisite performance of n***** melodies, is the veritable Leo Africanus— Robert Rose, Esq., the bard of colour.

[*Liverpool Standard* 1 July 1842]

It was during the period 1841–2 that Rose wrote poems on times gone forever, loss, despair, and his childhood home, in his notebook held by Chetham's Library. A period of deep mental anguish where some of the pages are covered in a wild illegible scrawl. While it was quite understandable that he should now want to 'take the waters' and try to relax, it was not quite so understandable that he should want these details to be a matter of public record. The *Liverpool Standard* was cruel and offensive (by modern standards) in their

THE CORONATION.

Awake! aspiring Muse, indulge one lay
To Britain's Queen, on this auspicious day!
Like incense, pour thy humble tribute forth
To her who rules the noblest land on earth.
Th' occasion's great, exalt my humble soul
With "thoughts that breathe" in melody to roll;
Pervade my mind till through th' electric frame
There dart a Patriot and a Poet's flame!
Thou who awok'st when ag'd Britannia's King*
Slept 'neath a greater monarch's powerful sting;
Thou who hast sung of stars and moon of yore,
And bathed in the deep stream of ancient lore,—
Awake! and sound the quivering string once more.
Oh, that to me were sent the gifts of song,
To rush in rapture like a tide along;
Then would I raise a glorious strain, I ween,
Fit for the ears of England's peerless Queen!
Then would such strain repay me with delight
For the bold wish to climb Parnassian height.
But vain this wish, for I have not the power;
I,—puny Minstrel of a passing hour,
Fearing to step before the public gaze,
To dare its censure or to court its praise,

* This refers to the Author's Elegy on the late lamented King, published in the *Sunday Times*.

'Coronation' poem (page 1) written and published for the coronation of Queen Victoria in 1838. (Courtesy of Chetham's Library, Manchester)

House of June

Come let us to the wild woods hie to-day
  Who'll miss a Bard
Who loves to walk in nature's grandeur
  And thinks it is hard
If he may not the scenes of nature see
Without the question asked "pray where is he?"

Let no one miss him from the busy scene
  And he will haste
Far from the vain the gay the cold the proud
  The scenes to taste

To A Man.

"... are not men who bear the name."

If thou art rich, let all thy kindness shine,
If thou art poor, learn poverty to bear,
If high and mighty, tread not on the low,
A very worm may turn a serpent foe.
In every station, act in such a way,
As will bring comfort at some future day.

If young, repress the warmth of passion's rage,
So that thou call not down reproof from age;
If old, still look with tenderness on youth,
Let thy experience be its guide to truth.
Let young and old still journey, hand in hand
Together searching for a better land.

Thus onward move, and through life's little span
Thus prove thy noblest claim, to be
  a Man. R Rose.

Above: 'House of June' a handwritten poem from Robert Rose notebook held by Chetham's Library. (Courtesy of Chetham's Library, Manchester)

Left: 'To a Man' a handwritten poem with a letter by Robert Rose held by Chetham's Library. (Courtesy of Chetham's Library, Manchester)

Child workers on
a sugar plantation
in the West Indies
c.1830.

Above left: Richard Cobden's house on Quay Street, Manchester used as an address by Robert Rose. (Courtesy of the author)

Above right: Site of Victorian lodging house at 18 Oxford Street, Manchester where Robert Rose lived c.1830s. (Courtesy of the author)

The Manchester Technical Schools. Robert Rose was very keen on further education for people, often helping to fundraise for institutions which provided evening classes.

Lines in his notebook addressed by Robert Rose to his friend Edwin Keet c.1840. (Courtesy of Chetham's Library, Manchester)

Right: Frederick Douglass 1818-1891, a freed slave who escaped from the American cotton plantations, and spent three months lecturing in Manchester in 1845.

Below: Manchester General Cemetery in Harpurhey where the grave of Robert Rose lies. (Courtesy of the author)

Above: Poet's Corner, Long Millgate, Manchester, opposite Chetham's College.

Left: The Sun Inn, Long Millgate, Manchester where the poets of Poet's Corner (Sun Inn) met.

Right: Portico Library members' reading room. (Courtesy of the author)

Below: Quadrangle with medieval buildings at Chetham's College, Manchester.

Chetham's College — Manchester

Above left: St Stephen's Street, Salford from the approximate position of the former No. 10 where Robert Rose spent his last years. (Courtesy of the author)

Above right: William Ewart, MP for Liverpool, friend and possible sponsor of Robert Rose.

Docks Board Offices, Liverpool, nineteenth century hub of world trade and commerce.

sarcastic dismissal of 'Leo Africanus' (African king) performing 'n***** melodies' on a ferry boat in Egremont, a town just 5 miles (8km) from Whitehaven, whether or not he was seriously considered to be Robert Rose. Rose had been on a northward-bound progress from Buxton through Fleetwood, Southport and Blackpool to Whitehaven, the town where he had first set foot on British soil, and perhaps the town from where he had hoped to leave British soil.

Chapter Twelve

'The chords of early life e'en vibrate still...'

As mentioned, during the period 1841–2 Rose wrote poems on times gone forever, loss, despair, and his childhood home. He was now approaching his late thirties with his ambitions of sailing the oceans, immortalising their fascination, wild majesty, and sense of adventure, to return to his much missed childhood home.

Departed Hours by Robert Rose, The Bard of Colour
Lonely I stand upon the mountain's site,
And gaze around me with intense delight;
What crowded visions, urged by fancy, rise,
Fantastically wrought in varied dies,
Then with the trembling twilight melt away,
As momentary vivid lightning's play
The fiery pinion sped, 'twere vain to trace
A vestige left is all the boundless space.
So, 'tis with thoughts wing'd from the human mind
Recall or trace their flight 'tis undefined,
Except dear memory lends her gentle aid,
And darts her radiance on the lengthening shade;
Swift as Aurora flings her cheering light,
At the prompt summons of this pleasing sprite,
They burst again upon the ravish'd sight.
But most of influence works when left alone
'Mid scenes of early youth – the enchanting tone

Of merry minstrels in the summer-morn,
Among the trees, and on the well-known thorn,

Beneath whose shade, ere mingling in life's care,
We welcom'd happiness with friends to share,
Is sweet and blissful, as the trees' spread boughs,
Recall the fervour of love's sacred vows,
Impressed upon young hearts when free from pain,
Which guileless deem'd such ties would firm remain,
As when their souls far from the mocking throng,
Caroll'd in unison love's mutual song!

What a brief space of time fled its round,
Since last I view'd those mountain-summits crown'd
With all the terrors of the storm's dread power!
Well I remember here my parting hour,
What contrast now, as each calm whisp'ring breeze
Sounds sympathetic of what once could please,
When every sprightly hour that fondly smiled,
Each miser glance of hoary Time beguiled –
When little prattlers join'd in games around; -
Ah! Will e'ermore their mirthsome tones resound!
And each gay opening scene, once careless view'd,
Lends wings of gladness to bright Hope renew'd;
At the fair glimpse of yon refreshing rill,
The chords of early life e'en vibrate still.
I cannot gaze beneath a glowing sky,
On mountain, hill, and dale, without a sigh.
(The History of Writing, p.380)

There are some much deeper issues here, some of which Robert Rose would have had the knowledge and the intelligence to have worked out and understood. The worst thing was that, even after abolition, persons of colour were still seen as second-rate citizens, in some cases even as third-rate citizens, regarded as completely inferior in very way to their former slave masters. Rose appealed time and again for equality in how people were seen and treated, claiming that all people are people under the skin, everyone a part of the human race. Sadly, nearly 200 years after his death, his appeal is still unanswered, his wish still unfulfilled. Rose's reflective wistfulness and nostalgia fills every line of 'Departed Hours' before he gives way to darker depths with 'Despair'.

> **Despair** (from his notebook held by Chethams)
> Lost on a turbulent and restless billow
> 'Mid fluttering hopes and cloudy galling days
> Phantoms of grief distract our weasy pillow.
> Despair's a friend mocks memory's by-gone days
> The elements of ocean, earth and air
> All shrunk aghast for lo! These came and found
> 'Tis thy hoarse voice fell demon grant despair
> The pestilential breath from cares abound
> Of damp and gloom hastles [*sic*] the throbbing world
> Then like a giant dost bestride the earth
> E'en now beheld by thy strong hand are curled
> The fairest joys mild hope had woke to birth
> The curses of all time with thee shall swell
> Deadly blighting foe – dark monsters sprung from hell.

His dreams shattered, there was no reason for Rose to remain in the huge trading port that was Liverpool. He could no longer play a part in his native country's future and he could no longer help fellow Africans and Creoles in Berbice to a better life. He gave up his day job through disillusion, not because he was simply lazy and frivolous. He may have chosen Manchester because, as well as a superior arts scene he may have felt that the cotton mill workers had more of an affinity with his ideals and beliefs.

He had been in England in 1819 when Peterloo took place, and was old enough to comprehend that the essence of what ordinary working people were asking for was more equality for all. They were marching for a fairer democracy and a fair day's pay for a fair day's work, both causes in line with Rose's beliefs. He would have been shocked at the outcome and the appalling injuries inflicted by slashing sabres, all of which the government of Lord Liverpool initially tried to deny. He would have recalled the outcome of the slave rebellion of 1763 in Berbice, which was entrenched in Berbice folklore, and the vicious punishments which followed. When beating slaves for misdemeanours, lashes of the whip were not supposed to exceed twelve, but the crueller masters could order up to a hundred lashes to be administered.

The realities of the slave trade, its horrors, cruelties and sheer injustice, its impact on the colonies, and the true story behind British imperialism and empire, are marginalised behind other issues which act as a smokescreen that, as David Olusoga eloquently put it:

> conceals the history of slavery and the slave trade behind a distorted and exaggerated memorialisation of abolition and ... presents the Industrial Revolution as a phenomenon that sprang wholly and completely from native British soil, but it is suspiciously silent about the source of much of the capital that funded and ... where certain key materials came from and who produced them.

Robert Rose would have managed to work out that his 'independent means' were almost certainly financed by profits earned from slave-based industries. It would have been a bitter pill to swallow. He may have not known the name of his father, but his father was a white man in the West Indies and would have have been connected to the sugar and cotton industries. It is also equally possible that the sponsorship by a Liverpool MP was a cover story for his independent means and why the actual details were a carefully kept secret.

The British are fond of saying that they were the first to abolish slavery. They were not. France abolished slavery in France and its colonies in 1794. Denmark and Norway abolished the African slave trade in 1803, Haiti abolished all slavery in 1804. In 1807 Britain passed the Abolition of the Slave Trade Act but did not abolish slavery in its colonies until 1833. Robert Rose, as a Classical scholar with a strong interest in history would have known of these dates which fell in, or just before, his own lifetime. As noted earlier, billions of pounds were paid in compensation to British slave owners; so much so that the final instalments were not paid until 2015. The slaves got nothing.

In 1841 Rose had chided his mentor and co-chair of the Sun Inn Poets, John Bolton Rogerson, for not encouraging him more to support the cause of abolition and emancipation through oratory as well as poetry. Rogerson was also editor of *Oddfellows Magazine* between 1841 and 1848, and in 1842 wrote 'A Friendly Tribute' to Rose in his volume of poetry 'From the Town'. He praised Rose's 'true and generous spirit', acknowledged his background and his poetic talent, paid tribute to their friendship, and in the final verse he embraces those of all creeds and colours:

> Give me the man, whate'er his race,
> Whate'er his creed or clime maybe,
> Who spurns at all that's low and base,
> And I will hold him kin to me:
> Oh, soon may all that moment see
> When prejudice no more shall reign,
> And all but love shall have departed!
> I hail thee, then, my friend, again,
> Thou kind, and frank, and liberal-hearted!

Rose responded with 'Fame, Freedom and Friendship', stating that 'this piece is intended as a poetic response to some lines addressed to me by Mr J.B. Rogerson, in his last work, entitled "A Voice from the Town and Other Poems"'.

Fame, Freedom and Friendship
Thou hast in kindness breath'd a strain to me,
Fain would I answer thee in words of flame;
Thou who most rich in gifts of Poesy
Has paid a tribute to my humble name:
My lyre, that has so long neglected hung,
Once more I strike, because t'is thou hast sung.
Thou sing'st that I am the first of India's land,
To touch the harp, and thou bidd'st me to tell
Some story bewitch'd by Fancy's magic wand,
And gleaming in the light of Reason's spell
Of that fair distant clime from which I came,
And strive to link it with my lowly name.

But thou forget'st to bid me to stand forth
As champion of all-gracious Liberty!
To join the spirit rising o'er the earth,
And bid America's dark slaves be free:
No more to crouch to the stern tyrant's nod,
But stand erect as men before their God!

Not only poets now can swell its voice
But orators, whose voice in thunder breaks,
Till the poor sons of slavery rejoice,
And every hill and listening valley wakes
With the loud cry of JUSTICE, TRUTH and LOVE,
Which angels echo from their thrones above.

High talents on this earth to few are given,
But all men can be kind and good and just,
And work in meekness out the ends of heaven,
To raise their fellow creatures from the dust,
To soothe the widow's woe, the mourner's pain,
Ah! Then my friend we have not liv'd in vain.

Yes! Few can track the lightening's fiery wing,
Like Franklin, or like Newton, dart afar
His mind o'er space, and the successful bring
Worlds in its scope, and measure star from star:
But goodness need not envy genius' power,
Genius too oft with misery for its power.

I'd rather have my tomb bedew'd at eve
With the lone orphan's, or the good man's tear,
Who softly stole at twilight there to grieve
And sobbed aloud THE FRIEND OF MAN RESTS
    HERE!
I'd rather have this quiet, humble fame,
Than hollow echo of an empty name.

What is this fame? precarious at the best-
A meteor-dream to float on others' breath,
A sea o'er which once tost, we find no rest
Until encircled by all-pitying death.
Oh! choose like me, the peaceful path of life
Far from ambition, parent of all strife.

[Oddfellows Quarterly, c.1840]

There is no evidence that Robert Rose ever sought out the company
of fellow African or West Indian groups of dark-skinned people, nor

is there any evidence that he read work by Black writers such Mary Seacole, Mary Prince, Louis Celeste Lecesne, Olaudah Equiano (who had given a talk in Manchester in 1790) or Ottobah Cugoano, all Black writers and abolitionists like himself, and all connected with the West Indies. The Quakers had opposed slavery for some time and were involved with Sons of Africa, a London-based group of Black abolitionists comprising freed slaves led by Olaudah Equiano and Ottobah Cugoano. A branch was subsequently formed in Manchester where there was a small Black population, although many of these were either African seamen discharged from ships in Liverpool or personal servants. One way of displaying wealth at the time was to have an African servant; and entries in the Manchester parish registers would seem to confirm this fashion.

St Anne, Manchester, baptism 17 February 1786:

> William Ballard a child now about Eight Years Old and son of the late William Tate late of the Isle de Las on the Winward coast of Africa. His mother also a native of that country [ref: Archives M403/1/1/2].

Manchester Cathedral, baptism 26 December 1798:

> Indiana Mundi aged 14, a negro girl from Congo on the coast of Africa, disposed of to Mr Paton at St Kitts and transferred from him to Archibald Paton M.D. [ref: MFPR 19, submitted by Mr George Dawes].

St Peter, Manchester, Mosley Street, baptism 1 October 1810:

> Thomas Stonehewer Travis a negro servant of Mr Travis an American merchant of North Carolina, born 1787 [ref: MFPR 164].

Manchester Cathedral, burial 9 March 1830 No. 279: 'a man of Colour Town's Yard' [ref: MFPR 15]. Manchester Cathedral, burial 26 August 1831 No. 933 Eliza Alburn of Manchester, aged 22 years 'a brown girl from Upper Germany' [ref: MFPR 15].

Rusholme St James: baptism 20 May 1842, No. 88 Phillip Birch Native of Congo Africa; burial 4 June 1842, No.10 Phillip Birch (an African) aged 27 of Victoria Park Rusholme. This man can also be found on the 1841 census as a 'Phillip Congo' [ref: MFPR 1817].

In 1788 a petition for the 'abolition of the trade in enslaved Africans' had been signed in Manchester. Despite the city's wealth being based on the textile industry, which relied heavily on African slaves, there was plenty of anti-slavery activism in the city as well as a strong Quaker influence. In 1807 the Abolition of the Slave Trade Act had been passed, although abolition and emancipation for existing slaves would have to wait for nearly another thirty years. Rose had been very passionate about the abolition of slavery in the West Indies, notably in British Guiana, and Sons of Africa would have been actively working towards the freeing of Caribbean slaves while Rose was in his teens and twenties. There is no record either of him being equally passionate about the remaining African American slaves on the North American continent, whose cause Sons of Africa was also supporting. Was it the North American slaves of whom he had been thinking when he chided Rogerson in 1841 over not actively encouraging him to be more vocal about abolition, because the Caribbean African American slaves were free men by that time? Given Rose's passion for the abolition and emancipation of slavery it is also surprising that there is no surviving reference by Rose to the visit of Frederick Douglass to Manchester in 1846.

Like Rose, Frederick Douglass was a Creole. He was born in Maryland in February 1815 to a Black mother and a white father;

although Douglass's mother was enslaved. Douglass was parted from his mother as an infant and she died when he was 7. He was taught to read by the wife of his master when he was 12, until his master decided that 'literacy would encourage enslaved people to desire freedom'. However, Douglass continued to believe that 'knowledge is the pathway from slavery to freedom' and secretly continued to teach himself. He eventually escaped from slavery in 1838 and in the safety of New York City he continued to work against the tyranny of slavery. After the publication of his autobiography in 1845 Douglass visited Britain, and in November 1846 he spoke at a meeting of the Anti-Slavery League at the Free Trade Hall in Manchester. It is almost inconceivable that Rose would not have wanted to meet him and offer support, but if he had done so, it is almost certain that he would either have written a poem about it, or that the newspapers would have commented on the Bard of Colour supporting the famous American abolitionist – doubtless with reference to Rose's impassioned anti-slavery speech of 1835. As with so much else about the story of Robert Rose, it is impossible to be definite, but the likelihood that the two men met is low, which in itself remains something of a mystery.

Frederick Douglass spent several months in north-west England during 1845/6. Rose's impassioned speech on abolition and emancipation had been published just ten years before Douglass's visit. Douglass was intelligent and well-read and he would surely have known of it and was likely to have read a copy. The speech had been reprinted over four times. Surely, he would have wanted to meet Rose. However, there was one major difference between the two men. Douglass had been born into slavery, had worked as a slave and suffered mistreatment as a slave, so he was passionately active in fighting for the abolition of slavery and the acceptance and equality of Black people. Rose certainly shared his principles, but he had been born a free man and had private independent means, which had almost certainly come from the white man's money earned from slavery. Perhaps he was forced to admit to himself that too much passionate protest could be seen as biting the hand that fed him. It would have been a bitter pill for him to swallow. Certainly, after the publication of his poem celebrating Queen Victoria's coronation in 1838 Rose seems to have confined his statements against slavery to his poetry. Possibly that might have been due to pressure from his unknown sponsor, but there are no clues. He wrote 'Fame, Freedom and Friendship', in 1840, the final poem that specifically refers to slavery, and from which poem his epitaph (below) was taken.

> I'd rather have my tomb bedew'd at eve
> With the lone orphan's, or the good man's tear,
> Who softly stole at twilight there to grieve
> And sobbed aloud THE FRIEND OF MAN RESTS
>   HERE!
> I'd rather have this quiet, humble fame,
> Than hollow echo of an empty name.

However, as we know, in 1841 Rose had complained to John Bolton Rogerson for not encouraging him more to support the cause of abolition and emancipation (of Black American slaves) through oratory as well as poetry. Why did he now need any encouragement? Why try to blame his lack of vocal support for the anti-slavery movement on Rogerson? That had not been the case in 1835 and by 1841 Rose no longer even had a day job to worry about. Douglass had certainly never needed any encouragement to fight against slavery and for the rights of Black men. He wrote volumes of autobiography on the topic, as well as giving numerous talks on the subject. This may explain a deep divide between the two men, and by 1846 Rose was drinking quite heavily so he might not have relished the possibility of having to defend himself to a man of Douglass's standing. Douglass was also an American and, although America had African slaves too, Rose had always been focused on African slaves in the West Indies who were by then liberated anyway.

Chapter Thirteen

'Land of my birth! Thy shores I long to tread...'

By 1843 there was a real sense that Rose's life was losing momentum. He had still not revisited his homeland. His great intended opus of the ocean remained unwritten. The Lancashire Literary Association, formed on 28 July 1841, faded as Prince, the principal figure of the group, Rogerson and another key member of the group moved away. The newspapers appeared fed up with him. It was a depressing time and he slipped into melancholy, doubtless accompanied by increased drinking. Although his poetry laments what he grieves, his emphasis has changed from focus on the slavery issue to poetry:

Home of my childhood by Robert Rose, the Bard of Colour
Home of my childhood thou art ever dear
O'er oceans sweet visions of thee come
Through the darkening changes of each rolling year
I fondly turn to thee, my far-off home.

At eve I oft direct my gaze above
To the pure beauty of each vesper star
Thou dost shine my early home of love
Thou art my light, soft glimmering afar.

My country! Although wrapt in mental night
For knowledge o'er thee scarce its ray hath spread

The Bard of Colour, Robert Rose

Can I forget where first I hailed the light?
Land of my birth! Thy shores I long to tread.

In thought my mother's voice chides dull delay
And lures me to my home, that long lost scene
But if again my footsteps there may stray
Say, shall I find it as it once hath been.

How dare I ask? when well I know the scythe
Of restless time is ever busy here
Perchance, and neath the thought the heart must writhe,
That mother hath departed from this sphere.

Ulysses erst before his kindred stood
A stranger at his mansion quite forgot;
How oft I muse in melancholy mood
And fear, like his, may be my mournful lot.

I sadly stand alone too oft to sigh
When pondering on that land so far away;
Alas! No kin are near me should I die,
There's none to soothe me in life's waning day.
A wanderer here, oh! for me who would mourn
If the vast sea of life should o'er me close?
Home of my childhood! May I safe return
To thee, then smiling sink to my repose!
So daily grows my craving wish to see My home
That I would almost dare the wave
On a frail plank, and risk my life as he
Whom e'en earth's conqueror admired as brave.

If offered here no other prospect fair
As a tired bird would seek its ark of rest,

To fold its weary wings – I'd hie me there.
To nestle in its bowers supremely blessed!

I, who left home in childhood, with changed form,
Will go to seek the spot of life' glad morn;
My mind will never bow unto the storm.
Long as home remains 'tis not forlorn.

In the still night amid the orange trees,
Or the tall palmy groves, I revel wild,
And hear the voice of love upon the breeze.
Once more in dreams a free and happy child!

I wake…the city's din comes o'er my soul,
In place of India's cataracts and streams;
Fleet as a rack the charm doth from me roll
Which lives for me but in my midnight dreams.

Just when my mother's voice I seem to hear,
And greet her honied accents kind and bland,
Too oft my smile is wedded to a tear,
To find I yet am in the stranger's land.

The Oddfellows Quarterly Magazine January 1842-October 1843
ODD FELLOWS' ANNIVERSARY. The members of the Veteran Lodge, Salford district, celebrated their anniversary on Monday evening, when upwards of 150 persons sat down to a sumptuous dinner. P.G. Wrigley officiated as chairman, and Mr Brownbill, surgeon, as vice-chair-man. The usual loyal toasts and others relative to the order were responded to in the course of the evening, with much spirit and enthusiasm.

Ald. Wilson Milburn made some exceedingly appropriate remarks upon 'The Independent Order'; and Mr J.B. Rogerson acknowledged the toast of 'The Editor and Committee of Management of the *Odd Fellows' Magazine*', congratulating the members of the order on the increase of talented contributors to the magazine, and mentioned, among others, Dr Bonling, who had sent a communication for the forthcoming number, and had announced his intention of continuing to be a contributor. 'The Strangers' was responded to by Mr Robert Rose, the bard of colour, who displayed more than his usual eloquence on the occasion, and made a very glowing and excellent contribution. The company was also addressed by R. Franklin, surgeon, F.D.G.M. Caldwood, D.G.M. Francis Smith, and others, with much effect. Messrs. Shepherd, Beswicks, Hargreaves, and others, favoured the party with some remarkably good vocal entertainment. The whole affair passed off spiritedly; and the conduct of the chairman obtained for him universal approbation.

[*Manchester Times*, Saturday, 16 December 1843]

INDEPENDENT ORDER OF ODDFELLOWS. The anniversary dinner of the Loyal Veteran Lodge of the M.U. Independent Order of Odd Fellows came off on Monday evening, at the house of host James Woolley, the Veteran Tavern Stanley-street, Salford. Upwards of 140 gentlemen and friends, 'put in an appearance' to our members we need hardly say, 'mine host's' better half occasion, when the entire effective strength of her buttery, exhibited in spread of viands almost unequalled in the gastronomic art, P.G. Thomas Wrigley occupied the post of honour and he was 'faced' by

Thomas F. 'Brownhill, Esq.' Among the company were noticed J. Rogerson, Esq., Editor of the Odd Fellows' Magazine, Robert Rose, Esq., the bard of colour, Dr Franklin Isaac Franklin, Esq., &c. &c. The cloth having been withdrawn, the usual loyal toasts were given, amidst loud applause, when the Chairman, after an appropriate Speech then commended the 'Order of Odd Fellows'. The toast was drunk amidst enthusiastic cheering P.G. William Melbourn acknowledged the sentiment. The next toast was the Widows and Orphans Fund, and may success continue to crown the Efforts of the Directors. P.P.G.M. Henry Ball rose, in answer to the call of the Chairman, and briefly addressed the company in support of the claims of this branch of the institution. The G.M. and Board of Directors met with a fitting response from P.D.G.M. John Caldwood. After some other toasts, the chairman proposed the Editor and Committee of the Odd Fellows Magazine. P.G.J.B. Rogerson rose and acknowledged the toast in a most eloquent address. The toast of 'The Strangers' called up Robert Rose 'Esq., the bard' of colour, whose address, we should think banished from the company the vulgar error of the islands being confined to the European race. After the toast of our worthy host, his wife and children, Mr Woolley, although labouring under serious indisposition from the effects of his late accident, stood up and briefly acknowledged the toast. It is beyond our power to give more than this brief sketch of the doings on this agreeable occasion. Everyone enjoyed himself and seemed to take delight in adding to the fund of mirth, and it was not till a late or rather early hour that the signal to our next merry meeting was given immortalis.

[*The Era*, Sunday, 17 December 1843]

Chapter Fourteen

'A cobbler's dancing with the Queen of Spain'

Rose had been in Manchester and Salford for Christmas in 1843, a period when, by his own admission, he had still not visited his former homeland. However, there was reportedly a silence from him during 1844/5, during which he is said to have gone travelling. It is quite possible that the 'period of silence' to which the *Manchester Times* had referred between June 1844 and October 1845, while Rose supposedly 'traversed the Atlantic and Pacific writing "The Ocean"', may not have been correct. It might be true that the newspaper did not hear from him during that period, but to date there is no proof that he ever actually left Britain. However, there is clear proof that Rose appeared to be in Manchester during the spring of 1845. On 29 April 1845 a fancy-dress ball was held at the Free Trade Hall on Peter Street in Manchester to raise money for public baths and wash houses in the city. Rose attended and subsequently wrote a long poem about the ball entitled 'The Festival of Fancy', which he dedicated to Charles Dickens. It was published in pamphlet form early that summer by George Falkner of King Street, the same company whom Rose would approach in 1848 about publishing a general volume of his work. Rose saw Dickens as a friend of the poor and oppressed and as such felt some empathy with him. Rose donated proceeds from the sale of his poem to the funds for the public baths and wash houses.

'The Festival of Fancy', although long (it ran to some fourteen pages) and written entirely in rhyming couplets, is a cheerful, amusing and light-hearted poem, unlike much of Rose's work, with some mischievous descriptions of costumes worn by those who attended. He begins:

> of light and music with its accents bland
> Vision a scene and breath of fairy land.
> Here wisdom, folly, sadness, joy, unite
> In groups fantastic to their ravished sight

Rose goes on to describe guests in costumes depicting Brutus, Caesar, Goths, Turks and Vandals, 'a wicked looking abbot … with a sly young nun', and, closer to his heart, 'a negro's hugging his vile chains in bliss; what would Wilberforce have said to this?' He mentions an 'ugly Desdemona', Napoleon asking Wellington if 'he'll take a glass of grog', Cromwell carving a piece of chicken for King Charles I, and Shylock chatting to the pope. Then he goes into full satirical mode:

> Peter the Great is whispering in mine ear,
> Newton is gazing at earth-stars, I fear,
> Peter and I, behold, and at Great Newton jeer,
> A cobbler's dancing with the Queen of Spain,
> A priest is sighing in lover's strain,
> A peasant's breathing to a fair Empress
> Soft hints of love and mutual happiness…

Subsequently, at the supper table, Rose descends into outright humour over scenes:

> here Sancho lustily bawls out for mustard,
> While Quixote daringly attacks a custard,
> Feeling no danger in this lavish treat
> And one is there delights to see them eat.

However, not everyone was amused and *The Era newspaper* (a Conservative newspaper 1838-1939 which took an interest in sport, theatre and the arts and was invaluable for reviews) clearly did not like either Robert Rose or his poem. Their review was harsh and unforgiving:

THE FESTIVAL OF FANCY. BY ROBERT ROSE, THE BARD OF COLOUR

The red rose and white rose are immortalised, and this poem, dedicated to Dickens, alias Boz, commemorative of the Fancy Dress Ball, in aid of the Baths and Washhouses' Funds, will, no doubt, apotheosise the black Rose. In these lovely tints we have depicted the phases at the Fancy Ball as they presented themselves to the 'Man of Colour'.

[*The Era*, Sunday, 8 June 1845]

Some of Rose's verses were then repeated and *The Era* pulled no punches:

Diogenes is here, an honest man
He looks! for, hath be with himself began?
A negro's hugging his vile chains in bliss;
Ah! what would Wilberforce have said to this?
Amazing sight the monster Caliban
In white kid gloves, picks up a lady's fan;
Socrates in a foolscap: and wise Solon,
So wise, indeed, he cannot point a colon.
Alexander seems a coward, and some jelly
Is stuffing into his luxurious belly
A Desdemona, ugly looks as sin,
Yet gay, almost, as with a glass of gin.
Bill Shakespere and Jack Sheppard are quite jolly;

Milton to them is bawling, 'Nix my Dolly'
Napoleon asks Wellington if he'll take
A glass of grog, if but for friendship's sake,
But Wellington says, 'no, 'twill make my head ache!'
Cromwell is carving Charles the First a slice
Of fowl, which Charles declares is very nice;
Peter the Great is whispering in mine ear
Newton is gazing at earth-stars I fear,
Peter and I, behold, and at Great Newton jeer.
A Cobbler's dancing with the Queen of Spain,
A Priest is sighing in a lover's strain
A Peasant's breathing to a fair Empress
Soft hints of love and mutual happiness!
Oh, motley group! Sailors who never saw
A sea, and Soldiers who ne'er sword did draw;
Rich Beggars and poor Kings, and Monks who ne'er
In convent mumbled forth a solemn prayer;
Philosophers whom reason would disdain,
And Poets who ne'er penned a single strain.

Would that our 'filthy bargain' had, Othello-like, recited his marvels in prose, to which even had any Desdemona listened she would have deserved to be smothered. Our Bard 'en noir', pours forth this mellifluous aphorism;

Let many a rogue or glad fool shuffle off
His character, for fear of scorn and scoff-
But with a character that shines star-fair,
To fall from any state what need we care?
Fortunately for the world, Rose has thus answered himself-
Our Addison has proved this moral sage,
In his great mount of ills, that pleasing page.

Still, in our daily walks, we love to ape
What is beyond us.
and we sincerely trust that he will profit by the last eight
words of his poetry alias his 'black art'.

[*The Era*, Sunday, 8 June 1845]

The *Manchester Times* eventually came to Robert Rose's rescue:

Mr Robert Rose, the Bard of Colour, has received gratifying letters in acknowledgment of his poems from, Charles Dickens, Esq., and T. Talford, Esq., among the guests invited to the Atheneum Soiree, and from other eminent literary characters. It will be seen by the advertisement that Mr Rose is now nearly ready with his long poem on the Ocean, careful and undivided attention to which has kept his Muse some time out of sight:

Knowledge shall yet progress from clime to clime,
And win the clarion praises of all time.

Note.—The above is in commemoration of a complimentary supper given to the author, by his friends in Manchester, which, in every respect, was an educational gathering.

[*Manchester Times*, Saturday, 25 October 1845]

Chapter Fifteen

'We alone are wandering...'

There is a period of just under a year (June 1844 – April 1845) during which Rose's movements are unaccounted for. This is the period when he supposedly 'traversed the Atlantic and the Pacific writing "The Ocean"'. There are no details of whether he worked a passage or paid for a berth, but he certainly talked about travelling the high seas on his return, and said he had a substantial piece of work to publish under the title of 'The Ocean'. While Rose may certainly have travelled the high seas it is doubtful that he ever actually left British waters. He could have sailed the Celtic Sea, the Irish Sea, the North Sea, the English Channel, and if he had sailed to the Western Rocks off the Isles of Scilly (28 miles south-west of Land's End) he would have found himself on the edge of the Atlantic Ocean. However, in the days of sail, at the mercy of winds and currents, it is unlikely he would have had sufficient time to sail the oceans as he had said he did and spend time in Berbice, but the actual reason for him not sailing the world or returning to the West Indies may be a little more mundane. In the 1840s travel abroad was not common and usually confined to the upper classes, except in the case of emigration, so there was no general passport system. Those who travelled, especially those of good social standing, carried letters of introduction signed by notable or influential people, to enable travel in foreign climes and to ensure safe passage. These travel documents would include name, surname, address, hair and eye colour, or unusual physical features, to make border crossings easier. Robert Rose would likely have faced a couple of major issues. His unknown sponsor may not have wished him to leave the country for various reasons, and Rose would then have experienced problems in obtaining appropriate documentation, and he might have risked his main means of support. Even if he hadn't, it might have proved difficult for him to actually access funds when he was out of the country. In any case, he knew that letters of introduction would be much more difficult for him to obtain than for most simply because he was Black. The other major problem for Rose, as a person of colour, was that although he might be allowed to leave England, there was a good chance he might not be able to return. He had no known contacts in the West Indies and he may have simply decided that the whole venture was just too risky.

In the event, 'The Ocean' was never published. The explanation given by Rose was that he had accidentally left his manuscript in a cab and it had been lost. In his notebook held by Chetham's Library there are a few notes and references to 'The Ocean' but nothing substantial. His explanation has flaws. If the manuscript was so important to him and represented the zenith of his life's work, he would hardly have left it abandoned in a cab – unless perhaps he was drunk. It might have been found, but it was not of any obvious commercial value so it was unlikely to have been stolen. Why did Rose not go straight to the firm from which he had hired the cab and search for it? He does not mention any search. He may not have searched for it at all. Perhaps he had been too drunk to remember where he left it and concocted the cab story to cover up the truth. At his inquest his landlady told the court that he had been drinking heavily for some time. Perhaps, if he had lived, Rose might have tried to rewrite his original ocean poem, and then finish it, but, if he did try, it has disappeared into history. Nevertheless, Rose did send an 'oceanic' poem to the *Manchester Times*, although seemingly before he left on his travels. It might have been a half-remembered fragment for his 'great opus'.

THE OCEAN: FROM AN UNPUBLISHED POEM BY ROBERT ROSE, The author of the following lines has not been before our readers for some time, having been engaged in his epic poem, entitled 'The Ocean', which has taken him often to its immediate vicinity, to avail himself of opportunities for the proper study of his subject. Having visited most of the watering places, besides having sailed over the Atlantic, the Pacific, and other oceans, Mr Rose may well be supposed to have taken his descriptions from Nature herself.

Here, at thy altars, Ocean, would I raise
To heaven's high King the hymn of love and praise;
How great must be his power who thee first planned,
And holds thee in the hollow of his hand.

On land we track o'er a dead world below,
On sea a living world beneath doth flow;
Advancing tides emblem man's rising race,
Receding tides can still retrace,
High islands are but the hill-tops from the plains,
And proudly rise from all thy rich domains;
Not only the hues of sun-set sky,
Or stormy billows, is changeful dye,
But in each part of this substantial globe
Thou putt'st on all around a various robe.
None ever clearly traced, or truly knew
The causes for thy tides and altering hue.
The lowing herd that perchance tide-turn
By instinct, true as reason given below,
Thy commune far extends above earth's graves,
To the high moon, the pilot of thy waves.

If any God appeared revealed in form,
Would it not be in the image of thy storm?
Planets at distance keep their eyes on thee,
Oft in the frenzy of thy revelry,
Like patient love that watches moonstruck madness
With silent sister's settled gaze of sadness.
Thou wagest war with land, invading still,
Its high domains, which yield to thy wild will;
Where empires flourish thou art revelling proud,
Trampling in stormy triumph o'er their shroud:
Thou art a living wonder ever rolling,
A death bell over empires ever tolling!

A glorious poem art thou! ever read
By passing ages as they deathward sped
A mighty book spread open to our gaze,
Filling the world with thy Creator's praise!

That like thine, loud Sea! a thunder-voice
Might shake the world, and bid all men rejoice
In Freedom, scattering chains unto the wind,
And swelling onward like a sea of mind,
Till LIBERTY triumphant over space,
Like thee, took all the world in her embrace!

The herd, however far from the sea, are described by some naturalists as knowing the exact turn of the titles; on which I will not hazard a decisive opinion, having attended more to the appearances on and around the ocean, than to anything of an indirect tendency to it. R. R.

[*Manchester Times*, 8 June 1844]

The *Manchester Times* were likely correct in their assumptions. Robert Rose, ever the man of mystery, left only tantalising glimpses rather than solid evidence of his travels. Of course, he may well have kept a travel journal or written poems which are now lost to us. In fact, from what is known of Rose himself, it is almost certain that he would have done so. However, all we really have is a fragment of what was supposed to be the culmination of his literary career and an undated poem written in the notebook held by Chetham's Library. It is certain there were other notebooks because the one held by Chetham's only contains about a quarter of his known output. In the Chetham's notebook there is a poem written around 1844 which is dedicated to a traveller. The first few lines indicate that he may have travelled during the later part of his life:

> **To a Traveller's Presence** (from his notebook held by
>   Chethams)
> All our early friends are dead
> We alone are wandering
> And walk on with solemn tread
> O'er their tomb-stone, pondering
> Thou hast travelled many a day
> Over sunburnt plains
> Where fierce tigers prowl for prey
> Where great horror reigns.
>
> Had thy travelling for thee won
> Peace of mind's expansion
> As the glory-joy to run
> To fame's summit-mansion.
>
> I have sailed o'er many a sea
> Where huge monsters reach

Down deep rivers infinity
This vast watery home
But I hope if settled down
Whether here or there
In the country as in town
I content shall share maternal
Yes content like mother's blessing
Whether good or wise
Whether sick or poor possessing
Is life's greatest prize.

Thou appeasest a wandering ghost
Thou art restless still
Ask them searching for friends lost
Gone by God's great will

As seekest thou in every clime
Remnants of the soul
By the great memory all divine
While the stars still roll.

Robert Rose might have intended to go travelling again, but trouble was brewing. European governments had been badly rattled by the events of the French Revolution (1789–99) and their implications. Their fears were justified when several revolutions broke out in Europe during 1848 which became known at the Year of Revolutions. This in turn impacted on American domestic and foreign policy because the Danish West Indies (Now the British Virgin Islands) and the French West Indies abolished slavery in the same year, which increased the general need for agricultural labour in the West Indies and stoked fears of abolition among the southern states of America. If Rose was keeping an eye on such matters he might have noted an item in the *Liverpool Shipping Telegraph* that HMS *Naiad* (named for a mythological Greek water sprite which would have appealed to his love of the Classics) was departing Liverpool on 29 July 1848, bound for Berbice under Captain William Rose. So far as is known the two men shared only a surname not a blood link. HMS *Naiad* was a fifth-rate frigate, a warship which had seen service at the Battle of Trafalgar, but by 1846/7 she was serving as a coal depot ship in Chile. The record then goes silent until she was recorded as serving in Peru around 1851. If she sailed to Britain in the spring of 1848 and then returned to the West Indies that summer, it is more than likely that she was recommissioned as a warship for four or five years until the international situation had quietened down. It is tempting to wonder if Rose did notice HMS *Naiad*'s proposed sailing to the lost land of his childhood, and perhaps he had even gone down to the docks to see the ship, probably intrigued that he shared an uncommon (in Liverpool and Manchester at that time) surname with the captain of the ship.

'And we, in sadness, must in vain deplore'

Mr Rose has probably written as much verse as any man in Lancashire, although yet, he never contributed to any very ponderous volume to the world of letters. It pleases us, however, to record the numerous little works that have emanated from his vigorous and industrious pen at different periods. In the first place we have a very pleasing 'Collection of Sonnets' which are highly commendable in both matter and style. They exhibit much excellence of feeling, and occasionally some free and flowing rhythm. Here and there we probably have some slight defects of metre and inelegance of diction, but, upon the whole, they betray some warm and noble emotions, boldness of conception and strength of expression. One or two of them have pleased us exceedingly, both for their fervency of emotion and melody of versification.

Another poem, entitled 'The Coronation', is a pleasing production, and manifests a goodly feeling of poetic flow and poetic utterance. We have read it with much satisfaction and can cordially coincide with the Countess of Blessington when she approvingly called it 'a very charming poem'. In some places, we must, impartially speaking, confess that he descends a little to the common-place, although this may probably have arisen from some haste or inadvertency in composition.

The poem has run through four editions, has been very generally read, and reviewed by most of the London and provincial papers in a laudatory strain. A beautiful copy of it was presented, through the present Earl of Carlisle, to her Majesty, the which she graciously received. It is a good specimen of the author's powers.

Upon the occasion of the Manchester Mechanics' Institution Bazaar, Mr Rose produced a very acceptable poem, entitled 'The Bazaar', which won the approval of the committee, and went through two editions. It is a somewhat pleasing performance; light and thrilling in versification, and warmly enthusiastic in matter. It was a pretty successful production and sold somewhat extensively.

A beautiful pathetic monody [poem lamenting a person's death] on the death of a young lady formed the subject of another production under the title of 'The Cypress Wreath'. Of this, the Countess of Blessington, who should be no mean authority, expressed herself as 'very much pleased with the perusal' and pronounced it 'well expressed, and written with great feeling and judgement'. With this we most cordially agree and consider the poem to be one of the best productions the author has brought before us. It is an utterance of grief in the most fervent sentiment, and is a feeling of poetry and language infused with its contents that cannot but enlist the sympathy of the reader. It is written with considerable ease of style and versification, and manifests throughout much of real poetry, both in the matter and the manner in which it is rendered.

Upon another local event, the Manchester Fancy Ball in aid of the Public Baths and Wash-Houses, Mr Rose again applied his pen in the production of a clever and pleasing little poem, entitled 'The Fancy Ball'. This, although possessing some flowing and musical versification, did not prove a very successful undertaking, although the object it had in view, and the general merit of the production itself, ought to have secured it a good share of public patronage.

Upon the whole, Mr Rose has fully maintained his claims as 'Laureate of the Isles'. His productions have been generally well received by the press, and among some of the higher authorities that have been pleased to eulogise them, we may mention Lords Brougham, Morpeth, Stanley, Russell, Lansdowne, Sydenham, with Charles Dickens, Moncton Milnes, Harrison Ainsworth, William Ewart, Joseph Pease, and other eminent literary and political characters.

[*Stockport Mercury* part of an article on Robert Rose written by John Evans, June 1849]

John Evans' article in the *Stockport Mercury* was taken in part from the longer article that appeared in the *Nottingham and Newark Mercury* which praised Rose's abilities:

The author of *Festus* has likewise acknowledged Mr Rose's genius in the following lines which appear here for the first time in print. It should, however, be observed in the preface, that Mr Rose has written a great amount of verse on the theme of the Ocean, and hence the manner in which we find him here addressed:

Bard of the Queen! Thou hast written well
On thine immortal theme; whereon shall dwell,
Ark-like and safe, thy fame. The years of time,
Are as a sea's waves; may thy noble rhyme,

With them flow on forever! For I find
In this the proof-strain of a strong high mind,
Beauty and power, and music like the seas,
And deep sublimity; and more than these,
A love of wave like freedom, and a soul,
Full of kindness for the human whole.
Therefore thou shalt have honour in man's tongue
Wherever ocean rolls or song is sung.

Beside the productions named, Mr Rose has been a long well-known contributor to the Literary Gazette, Monthly Magazine, Weekly Dispatch, Sunday Times, Liverpool Albion and Mercury, the York, Bath, Bristol, Preston newspapers, and most of the Manchester ones. In a small collection of local poetry under the euphonious title of *The Festive Wreath* we find a fine and somewhat vigorous poem entitled *Fame, Freedom and Friendship*, which we have read with considerable pleasure. We understand Mr Rose has another work in the press, under the pleasing title of *Visions on Sea and Land*. From what we have seen of Mr Rose's recent productions, and from what we know of his natural ability, this work will doubtless prove the best hitherto published by him.

After quitting school he was occupied in a commercial house in Liverpool, and seen in another of the same description in Manchester. At this period it was his intention to return to his native soil, and placing himself in these houses he was desirous to acquire some general knowledge of the nature of conducting commercial affairs, in these two good marts. But the 'thraldom' (as he termed it) of commerce did not suit his taste, and possessing an easy competency, he, as he has observed, 'preferred the peaceful and pleasing paths of poetry to the desire of gain and the turmoil of business'. Throughout his life Mr Rose has advocated the cause of freedom in contradistinction to negro slavery, with unabated zeal, although such a course was in direct opposition to his own personal welfare. He has often stood alone to advocate the claims of this great cause and has fought the noble battle with the most laudable perseverance. At the Brougham dinner in Liverpool, in 1835, Mr Rose delivered a very animated and eloquent speech. During his speech he was frequently interrupted by some anti-abolitionists; but he maintained his ground and came off the entire conqueror. His speech upon that occasion has been printed in pamphlet form and presented him by the committee. Mr Rose has frequently addressed large assemblies in Liverpool, Manchester, and other neighbouring towns. He has likewise delivered a series of lectures upon poetry, which were considered able and interesting.

[John Evans's article in the Nottingham and Newark Mercury which praised Rose's abilities]

When Robert Rose read the whole article several witnesses reported that he became badly upset, angry and agitated, repeatedly crying out 'It's a comedy! It's all a comedy!' and to which the poet took great exception for reasons never made clear. Even John Evans was puzzled, because he had written nothing that could be deemed condemnatory. However, the *Mercury* continued, 'in a communication which we have recently received from Mr George Richardson, the author of "Patriotism &C" he has observed "I am glad to learn that Robert Rose said the biography was good..."'

Although initially mystifying as to why Rose should react that way to an article which was detailed and mostly flattering in its content, it must be remembered that the article was published just two or three weeks before his death, when he was already drinking heavily and his experiences had caused him to become cynical about life. His youth was gone. His ambition had failed. His days with the Sun Inn Poets were over. His major work, 'The Ocean', had been lost. His poetry had not been published as a volume, like many of the other Sun Inn Poets, so he had not received the recognition he might have felt was due. His skin tone was still attracting unwelcome remarks. Therefore, when Rose read the article lavishly praising his talent, and even his genius, as a poet, he felt that he had little to show for it and that he was not fully appreciated solely due to a simple accident of birth. It was just too much for him and he lashed out. His mood was as bleak as the opening line of 'Winter', a sonnet he had written a few years before.

WINTER. BY ROBERT ROSE, A WEST INDIAN OF COLOUR.

OLD Winter frowns upon the skies once more;
At his shrill voice how changed each outward scene,
And we, in sadness, must in vain deplore
Bland Summer's vanish'd flowers and fields of green.
While the lone soul retires within itself…

Chapter Seventeen

'The friend of man rests here. I'd rather have this quiet humble fame...'

There is a melancholy epitaph on Robert Rose's gravestone now hidden from general view in a discreet corner of a Manchester cemetery:

> I'd rather have my tomb bedew'd at eve
> With the lone orphan's or the good man's tear
> Who softly stole at twilight here to grieve
> And sobb'd aloud — the friend of man rests here
> I'd rather have this quiet humble fame

Transcript of the inquest: Melancholy death of Mr Robert Rose, the well-known bard of colour.
There are few people in this locality among those who occasionally revel in the fields of poetry, who have not heard of Mr Robert Rose, the 'bard of colour', whose lyrics and poetic effusions have at least gained him some notoriety, if they have not brought him fame. He has been a resident in Manchester some 14 or 15 years, and during that period has contributed to the poets corner of many of our local newspapers, besides figuring as the author of some small poetic tomes. Yesterday, he breathed his last, under the most melancholy circumstances, the victim of an over-wrought excitement, induced and strengthened in habitual intoxication.

According to the evidence adduced at the inquest held on his remains yesterday, before Mr Henshall, deputy coroner of the Duchy of Lancaster, in Salford, it appeared that the unfortunate man, who is about 43 years of age, was a native of Berbies [Berbice], in the West Indies, and some 15 years ago he was sent to this country by his father, a man of considerable property, to learn the Manchester trade. Disliking business however, and being possessed of sufficient means, he gave himself up entirely to literary pursuits and led the life of a gentleman.

Mrs Fentem, a widow lady with whom he lived in St Stephen Street, Salford, says that some time ago his habits became very irregular, and he frequently abandoned himself to fits of intoxication which latterly became more frequent. If not indulged with all he wanted he would get into a very excited state and was only provoked to further indulgence unless his whims were gratified.

Within the last few days he had a fit of this kind, and on Saturday evening last drank a pint of whisky, a pint of brandy, two quarts of ale and three bottles of porter. He had not been in bed for seven or eight days, but had sat drinking all night through, and since Friday had never tasted food in the house. The servant fetched him more drink on Sunday morning.

Police Constable Williams said that he had had considerable trouble with the deceased on Monday evening and early on Tuesday (yesterday) morning, having met him close to his lodgings several times in a very excited state of mind. On two occasions he induced the deceased to go into his lodgings and remain quiet.

About a quarter to three o'clock he again met him in Kirkley Street, carrying a bedroom candlestick and a box of matches in his hand, and apparently going towards the police-office, when he spoke to him, and desired him to go home and get to bed. The deceased began to talk in a very unintelligible way about the *Stockport Mercury* – occasionally ejaculating 'It's all a comedy; I say it's all a comedy.'

Satisfied of his insanity, he took him to the police-office, when he commenced repeating snatches of poetry, and began to undress himself as if to get into bed. On finding himself detained, he asked for a pint of ale, which witness told him was not allowed, but he was told that if he wished for a jug of tea or coffee, it should be fetched from his lodgings. This he refused to allow and then fell down on his knees and began to pray.

At about six o'clock witness visited him again, and found him still praying on his knees, but he remained resolute and refused to let either tea or coffee be fetched for him. Witness could not then tell what the deceased meant by the *Stockport Mercury*, but he had since asked Mrs Fentem, who said there had been something in that paper about his poetry, which had preyed very much on his mind. [One of the jurors here said 'why there was a portrait of him in the *Stockport Mercury* a short time ago'.]

Inspector Brown said he constantly visited the deceased in the lock-ups from six to eight o'clock that morning, when he appeared to be raging mad. He kicked at the door of his cell, and shouted for water until he was hoarse, when witness took him water and entreated him to keep quiet. At nine o'clock he was brought out of the lock-ups, and taken to the courthouse before the magistrates, when, they seeing his state of mind, ordered him into the lock-ups again until he could be taken to the workhouse.

On being re-conducted to his cell he became exceedingly violent and struggled with the officers, making some ineffectual attempts to bite them. At a quarter before ten o'clock witness visited him again when he found him standing upright, violently gesticulating and talking to himself; but before witness left him he threw himself on the floor, and, seizing the leg of a form or bench, made several convulsive attempts to force the lock-up door with his feet. At ten o'clock witness again visited him when he still lay on the floor but appeared more quiet and seemed to breathe more easily and regularly. About a quarter of an hour later (having in the meantime got an order for his removal to the workhouse) witness again went to see him, when he found him lying quite still on the floor, grasping the leg or form, but quite dead.

Mr Neal, chief constable, said, that having been told by one of his officers that he feared the deceased was dying, he sent off for surgical aid instantly, hastening himself to visit the unfortunate man in the interim. When the surgeon (an assistant of Mr Edge's) arrived he declared that life was quite extinct.

This being the whole of the evidence, the coroner briefly addressed the jury, who, without deliberation, returned a verdict of 'Death from excessive drinking' which the coroner dutifully recorded.

Although Robert Rose lived and died in Salford it was decided that he should be buried in the Manchester General Cemetery, which had opened just off the Rochdale Road in Harpurhey in 1837. It was not consecrated ground until 1888, when a Church of England chapel was built in the grounds so there are no parish register records for burials before 1888, and any records from the preceding fifty years have either been lost or destroyed. However, Robert Rose was listed as a Non-Conformist burial in plot 6087. The actual site is uncertain but was almost certainly in the area of graves from a similar date which lie to the left of the Rochdale Road entrance. His gravestone was finally recovered in 2012 and revealed his epitaph to be a quote from one of his own poems 'Fame, Freedom and Friendship', written as a poetic response to some lines addressed to Rose by John Bolton Rogerson, in his work, 'A Voice from the Town and Other Poems', written in 1842. In order to protect the gravestone from the elements and souvenir hunters it has been placed under the shelter of a hedge and covered over with turf. John Bolton Rogerson was the registrar for the cemetery in 1849 when the interment of Robert Rose took place and it was probably he who chose the site for his fellow poet and friend. St Stephen's Church (1794–1956) in Salford was just across the way from where Rose lived on St Stephen's Street and his burial there might have been more logical. In any case, Salford is not just a different parish, it is a different city to Manchester, separated from it by the River Irwell. Rogerson would have had to pull some strings, but he knew Rose well enough to know that downtown industrial Salford was not a place that he would ever have chosen to rest for all eternity. Rose's mind, right to the end of his life, was filled with thoughts of the natural world. One of his last published poems, in May 1847, was called 'Public Parks'.

Public Parks
The heavens declare the glory of their God!
His skill alone could spread the verdant sod;
He only could adorn the simplest flower.
That glows through every summer-sabbath hour.
Survey His wondrous domes where grand.
Vast temples reared by no mortal hand

Behold the humblest flowers, the loftiest trees;
Was Solomon arrayed like one of these
Far dart thy mind's eye
Or Ocean, and then lift
To the bright stars that
Twinkling through windows of the arching skies.
Then praise the wise and philanthropic plan
Which, raising, purifies, the heart of Man.

Rogerson could not give Rose his beloved ocean, but he could give him his public park. The Manchester General Cemetery was built away from the city centre millscapes in Harpurhey, which, in 1830, was described as 'having pleasant views', and stood next to Queens Park, opened in the summer of 1846, with which it eventually merged. It is quite possible that Robert Rose had walked in Queens Park, had seen the new General Cemetery, had maybe mentioned to his friend, the registrar, that it would be a good place to be buried, given that he knew he would never return to Berbice.

A footnote of irony is that Robert Rose believed that lack of education was a major cause of crime so he had visited Salford Sessions, adjacent to the jail where he would die just ten years later, and written about the criminals he had seen there on trial:

**LINES WRITTEN ON SEEING THE CRIMINALS
AT THE SALFORD SESSIONS.**
How humble are those who were late so bold
In bartering virtue for the sake of gold!
Before their judge they bend with faces meek,
Fear in their eye and shame upon their cheek.
They seem repentant, and kind mercy seek,
Which, like the rainbow, still may brightly span
The darkest doom of sinful, erring man.
No heart's so callous but the tender ties

Of love and friendship claim close sympathies!
To be transported, and, perchance, for life,
From fondling children and an anxious wife,
Must give them torment long before the time
That sentence is pronounced upon their crime.
'Tis pleasing, in one sense, to view the state
Of laws on those whom punishments await,–
Because they give security to those
Who else would know no safeguard from their foes.
Subduing evil passions, order reigns,—
This general perquisite the public gains.
But, in another sense, 'tis painful still
To view the crimes that do our records fill!
To know that Ignorance is the blackest cause
Of bold infringements of the nation's laws!
Let Education, then, spread far and wide,
And flow around like a refreshing tide!
That all may drink of Knowledge, taste of peace,
And crime and discord may for ever cease!

    [23 April 1839, ROBERT ROSE, the Bard of Colour.
        Published by the *Liverpool Albion*, 30 April 1839]

Chapter Eighteen

'Oh, had misguided men proved less unkind...'

Discrimination is a disrespect of differences and a rejection of individuality. People can be harshly judged on grounds of ethnicity, colour, religion, disability, gender, class, income, education and a raft of lesser causes. Rose certainly suffered his share of racial taunts and prejudice, even from his friends, a fact which Charles Kenworthy picked up on in his poem. 'Oh, had misguided men Prov'd less unkind, he'd been himself again!' However, there is no evidence that Rose was banned or shunned on account of his creed or colour. It may simply have been that, because he was educated and had private means, he was accepted and welcome in Chetham's Library; the Portico; the Manchester Literary and Philosophical Society; the Sun Inn Poets circle; as a public lecturer on poetry; and he could dine or drink when and where he chose; but it displayed a certain measure of acceptance by Mancunians not always evident elsewhere. Although he never married, Rose was often seen with a pretty white girl on his arm without comment. Compare and contrast with a personal experience in modern-day America, where white Americans still feel free to ask white strangers why they are in the company of coloured strangers. Rose believed in the equality of all human beings, as he made crystal clear in his speech at Lord Brougham's 1835 dinner, and challenged anyone who contradicted that notion. He had continued working for the 'mercantile house' in Liverpool where, if Evans was correct, he had determined to learn about trade, economics and markets; or, if Evans was not correct, in some other profession; so that he could one day return home and help his fellow countrymen find new lives. He thought that day had arrived in 1833 when slavery in the West Indies was officially abolished, but he had tragically misread the mindset of the British Empire. However, this does not fully explain the hidden catalysts in his life which turned Robert Rose from a sociable, idealistic and passionate young man into a lonely, cynical, hard-drinking older man. If Rose himself ever chose to explain it, that explanation has not survived, so we are left trying to piece together workable suppositions. His poems can be interpreted in a dozen different ways, or not at all. Poetry was his chosen means of expression. It may be significant that although he wrote a great deal about death and the grave, which were gloomy and oppressive subjects, though talked about much more in Victorian England than today, he could not face the reality of them. He could not bear to be with friends who were terminally ill and watch them die. Not knowing if his mother was alive or dead was almost certainly a significant factor in his decision not to return to his homeland.

Until recently the facts of Robert Rose's life for the first thirty years of his existence could be summed up in a couple of sentences. He wasn't a shy or retiring sort of person, as several eye-witness accounts testify, but he was very coy about his personal circumstances. Details were sparse to the point of non-existence. Even towards the end of his life, when he was drinking heavily and could be unpredictable, he never let slip personal information about his background, his family, his childhood, or his travels. He did not talk much about his feelings, using his poetry as a medium, but much of it reads as third hand, not first hand, experience, sometimes stilted by his insistent use of rhyming couplets. If he kept a diary or a journal, they have not survived. The notebook held by Chetham's contains mostly poetry, or notes relating to poems and publication, but only covers a period of four or five years (c.1840–4). His social life, events he attended, causes he supported, are mostly detailed through the words and comments of others, so again, he is usually referred to in the third person. Even when Rose himself is writing letters to newspapers he rarely gives a proper address, just the name of the town from which he writes. He is a man of mystery, and it is difficult to get a sense of the person he really was.

The only time Rose's real voice is heard is in the speech he gave on abolition and emancipation in 1835, a subject about which he was passionate and challenging, but he had enough intelligence to realise that, for a Black person to be living the lifestyle of a gentleman in Victorian England, he needed to keep many of his true feelings under cover. So he did what many do to mask their pain or anger, and hid behind a mask of smiling bonhomie and hospitality; genial and friendly to his fellows, charming to the ladies. He had the speech he gave in Liverpool printed in pamphlet form, and it sold well, but he never followed it up and so it gradually lapsed into obscurity. As noted earlier, today – 175 years after his death – there is not a single copy of the speech available on public access in England, so thanks again to the National Library of Australia in Canberra for allowing their copy to be digitised and included in this book.

It is ultimately very ironic that, a couple of years after publication of his speech on slavery, he wrote a poem for the coronation of Queen Victoria in which he praised, honoured and complimented the queen of the very empire that had inflicted the nightmare of slavery on the African and Indian nations. It is tempting to wonder if he secretly cringed with curling toes as he penned his lines of adoration for Victoria. If Rose had been a lesser person, cold and calculating his best chances, it would have been easy to dismiss him as simply taking advantage of the situation, but he was not that sort of person. He truly believed in equality for everyone. He never met the queen, but he ascribed to her all kinds of positive physical and personality virtues that he thought fitting for her role as queen of the British Empire (for which he was criticised by some), and then let his imagination go to work. The queen was still an impressionable teenage girl, still naïve enough to be simply flattered by all compliments without questioning them, and she let it be known that his coronation poem was pleasing to her. Rose was delighted that she liked it, but also relieved because he had come to understand that his options were limited after realising he could no longer return to the Caribbean.

However, it took the aftermath of death for Robert Rose to become less of an enigma. He might have died alone and an alcoholic, but he received the usual commemorative notices that the recently deceased are wont to command, and it is only then that the first indications of what he actually looked like were published. How different it might have been if he had lived in the age of social media, but Robert Rose died on the cusp of the photographic age, which began around 1850, and there are no known drawings, paintings or lithographs of him – which is perhaps unusual, considering that he was 'a person of colour', although Manchester was not then a multi-cultural city. In the *Nottingham and Newark Mercury* of 15 June 1849 John Evans wrote:

In private company he is an extremely pleasant and agreeable companion, full of wit and anecdote and evidently conversant with all the details of literature. As a man he is warm, hearty, and hospitable in the fullest degree. He presents a pleasant personal exterior. He is somewhat stout in build, and a little above middle height. His face is round in conformation, and his complexion of an olive hue. His forehead is rather finely developed, and his full dark eyes are beaming and expressive.

[John Evans, *Nottingham and Newark Mercury*,
15 June 1849]

There is also another physical description of him given by J.C. Bates, an engraver and artist who worked for the *Buxton Advertiser*. As a young man he had lived in Manchester in 1838/9 and wrote:

> I used to see Robert Rose at the house of Henry Wilmot Jones in St Stephens Street, Salford, where also dwelt Philip James Bailey, the author of Festus. At this house also I first became acquainted with John Bolton Rogerson (Rose's fellow poet and registrar at the new Harpurhey cemetery) ... there also came, sometimes on Sundays, Mathew de Pere, a scholar and a gentlemen; and there too I met and smoked my first pipe with the Rev. Patrick Ross of the Scottish church ... occasionally would come David Ross (an historian), brother of Patrick, of the Liverpool Chronicle.

Mr Bates had then added that:

> Robert Rose was a good-looking well-built man of a mulatto (mixed African and European parentage) complexion. The conversations were bright, witty, and animated, and often produced some good laughs.
>
> [*Manchester Notes and Queries*,
> Vol. Vi, 13 June 1885]

J.C. Bates's description of Robert Rose tallies well with that of John Evans who wrote about the poet two weeks before Rose died and chimes well with accounts of Rose's visits to Chetham's Library, when he was often in jovial mood with a girl on his arm.

In the same volume of *Manchester Notes and Queries*, a week earlier on 6 June, Joseph Johnson had written from Douglas in the Isle of Man:

> From some source, when he attained a man's estate, he became independent of labour, and was therefore not a

poor poet … although a poet of means and emulous of fame, he never published a volume of poetry.

He then went on to say:

> Rose, having a competency and having no necessity to 'drag at the oar' unfortunately dimmed his capability for work by too free and too frequent self-indulgence … ultimately his mind became affected, not so much by free living, as by free drinking … adding one more instance of the many and continually occurring instances of perverted and destroyed genius through the fascination of drink.
>
> [*Manchester Notes and Queries*, Vol. Vi, 6 June 1885]

The following week, on 27 June, in the same volume of *Manchester Notes and Queries*, someone giving his initials only as T.F.M., from Avon Street in Chorlton-on-Medlock, responded to Joseph Johnson about the question of Rose never publishing his work:

> Mr Joseph Johnson is correct in stating that Mr Rose never published his poems in book form, but I believe that in 1848 he was intending to, as I remember seeing him on several occasions at the printing office of the late Mr George Falkner, then of King Street, and in whose employment I was; and I have a distinct recollection of a specimen page of his poems being set up in type … a very common practice previous to publication.
>
> [*Manchester Notes and Queries*, Vol. Vi, 27 June 1885]

Those writing in the *Manchester Notes and Queries* seemed to have a personal knowledge of Robert Rose, which is perfectly possible as the entries are written just thirty-five years after Rose's death and would place the writers in their late sixties or very early seventies. Mr Bates and T.F.M. both refer to having known Rose in the last decade of his life when they were clearly just starting out on their careers. Joseph Johnson was more formal, but he certainly had personal knowledge of Rose. He writes, 'From some source, when he attained a man's estate, he became independent of labour', which would suggest that Rose began to receive his annual income of £300 when he attained his majority (came of age). This would normally have been when he reached the age of 21, in or around 1827. It makes more sense than his coy insistence that he was being funded by a mysterious Liverpool MP; but then again, truth is often stranger than fiction. Johnson also lamented that the 'Ocean Mystery' was not finished when Rose died and he quotes a sonnet written by Rose as showing his considerable talent:

> To thee, thou splendour of the night's ebon scene,
> Deep, silent orisons are swiftly pour'd
> From pious hearts, all lonely and serene,
> As incense pure, ascending to their Lord,
> At this dread hour, immers'd in reverie deep,
> Holding still converse with thy ray afar,
> A wilderness of thoughts which banish sleep,
> Distracts the mind, and wings it, glorious star!
> Up to the centre of the universe
> To wander there, in space of spheres sublime;
> But still think calmly on the quiet hearse,
> What hour it slowly moves to church-bell's chime:
> Though earth it bears to earth, yet, like thy light,
> The soul shall rise resplendent o'er its night.
>
> [Robert Rose, date unknown]

More intriguing, however, is J.C. Bates contribution to the memory of Robert Rose. He paints a tantalising picture of cosy literary soirees on Sunday afternoons in the house on St Stephen's Street, Salford, belonging to Henry Wilmot Jones, who was known as a 'publisher of provincial poetry'. Jones's housemate was Philip James Bailey, whose celebrated poem, 'Festus', much admired by Tennyson, was published in 1839. Also in attendance was leading Sun Inn Poet, John Bolton Rogerson; the scholar, Matthew de Pere; and the Rev. Patrick Ross, of the Church of Scotland, occasionally joined by his brother David who worked for the *Liverpool Chronicle*. These meetings were an interesting mix of family and artistic friends. In 1840 Henry Wilmot Jones wrote and published 'Manchester as it maybe … inland bonding', which was a well-researched and detailed proposal for what would become the Manchester Ship Canal so that Manchester could have port status alongside London and Liverpool, and would therefore be entitled to have bonding warehouses. Bonding warehouses are secure facilities for holding and storing goods liable to import duty and enable payment of customs duties to be deferred until the goods are sold or removed from the bonded warehouse. It could very well have been a bonding warehouse for which Rose worked before he left Liverpool. Henry Wilmot Jones had married Robina Ross in 1830. David Ross and the Reverend Patrick Ross were her brothers. Philip Bailey was gratified that Rose had bought the first copy of 'Festus' to be sold as this had greatly encouraged further sales for him. John Bolton Rogerson had written 'A Voice from the Town' and ran the Sun Inn Poets in Long Millgate along with Robert Rose. Conversation was lively and interesting and the young J.C. Bates paid close attention, so that he was able to say that he saw no evidence of the drinking which marred Rose's later life.

During his lifetime Robert Rose had many of his poems published separately, a good number of them in newspapers, a few in pamphlets, and one or two in collections of the work of others. In the years since his death it has been commented that it is strange that there is no published collection of his own work. T.F.M., a young printer's apprentice in 1848, stated that Rose was fully intending to have a collection of his work published and had gone so far as to be seriously considering this project with printer George Falkner, presumably the employer of the young T.F.M. This was about three years after the failure of Rose to complete his great opus on the Ocean for publication, the draft of which was then lost. Rose lamented its loss greatly, but made no effort to replicate the poem, although he must have remembered large chunks of it. Possibly his by now heavy drinking had affected his memory. Charles Kenworthy, in his volume on 'Original Poems on Miscellaneous Subjects' (1850), wrote some lines on the death of Robert Rose:

> Warm were his feelings and his tastes refin'd
> His country's weal engaged his ardent mind;
> Oppression's foe, the friend to liberty!
> Slave-torturing Africa, he sung of thee;
> The Bard, indignant at her horrid trade,
> Stood nobly forth the negroes cause to aid.

He then continued and addressed the problem of Rose's excessive drinking:

> One fault him swayed with fascinating tone,
> A spell that did his reason oft dethrone.
> Peace to the Bard! Oh, had misguided men
> Prov'd less unkind, he'd been himself again!
> Ye strict in morals, cease his worth t'assail,
> While pity o'er his frailty draws the veil.

Kenworthy's poem neatly explains the problems and the ultimate tragedy which beset Robert Rose during his lifetime. The causes of what turned him to drink are not definite, but not difficult to work out. He was lonely, with no one close to whom he could turn for comfort, or in whom he could confide his problems. As he lamented, even his family were absent from his records, and would be from his graveside. However, one word can sum up a major problem in the life of Robert Rose. Discrimination. From his speech at the Liverpool dinner of 1835 to the end of his life, Rose passionately and volubly protested the notion that people of colour were, by definition, inferior. Racial prejudice remains a serious problem today, despite continuing educational and legal efforts to ensure equality. We are all people under the skin, and skin hues should not matter, but they do, sometimes even more so in recent times. There is still living memory of Black people and white people being segregated in different rooms or in different places, and of bans on inter-racial marriages.

The lines from 'Black Lament' written by Langston Hughes in 1924 could well have applied to Rose's mother:

I am the child they stole from the sand
Three hundred years ago in Africa's land.
I am the dark girl who crossed the wide sea
Carrying in my body the seed of the free.

James Baldwin, an African American poet, novelist and playwright was born in that same year of 1924. He too defended Black people vociferously and spoke out about racism.

'Please try to remember,' he said, 'that what they believe, as well as what they do and cause you to endure, does not testify to your inferiority, but to their inhumanity.' How wise his words and how well they would have resonated with Robert Rose.

Appendix

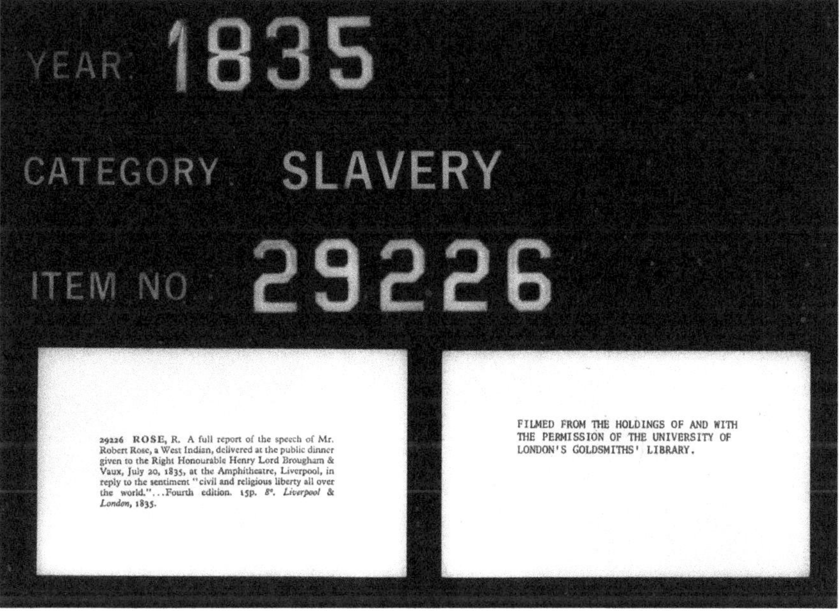

29226 ROSE, R. A full report of the speech of Mr. Robert Rose, a West Indian, delivered at the public dinner given to the Right Honourable Henry Lord Brougham & Vaux, July 20, 1835, at the Amphitheatre, Liverpool, in reply to the sentiment "civil and religious liberty all over the world."...Fourth edition. 15p. 8°. *Liverpool & London*, 1835.

FILMED FROM THE HOLDINGS OF AND WITH THE PERMISSION OF THE UNIVERSITY OF LONDON'S GOLDSMITHS' LIBRARY.

Full text of abolition and emancipation speech given in Liverpool by Robert Rose, July 1835. (Courtesy of the National Library of Australia in Canberra)

University of London
The Goldsmiths' Library.

A
FULL REPORT

OF THE

SPEECH OF MR. ROBERT ROSE,

A WEST INDIAN,

DELIVERED AT THE PUBLIC DINNER GIVEN
TO THE RIGHT HONOURABLE

HENRY LORD BROUGHAM & VAUX,

JULY 20, 1835,

AT THE AMPHITHEATRE, LIVERPOOL,

IN REPLY TO THE SENTIMENT

"CIVIL AND RELIGIOUS LIBERTY ALL OVER THE WORLD."

PUBLISHED BY A SUBSCRIPTION OF WEST INDIANS IN THIS TOWN,
AS A TESTIMONY OF RESPECT TO THEIR COUNTRYMAN.

Fourth Edition.

LIVERPOOL:
PRINTED AND PUBLISHED BY E. SMITH AND CO.,
LORD-STREET;
SOLD BY LONGMAN AND CO., LONDON; WILLMER AND SMITH,
AND J. WALMSLEY, CHURCH-STREET; ROCKLIFF AND
DUCKWORTH, CASTLE-STREET, LIVERPOOL;
AND BY ALL BOOKSELLERS

1835.

PRICE TWO PENCE.

'A Full Report of the Speech of Mr Robert Rose, a West Indian. Delivered at the public Dinner given to the Right Honourable Henry Lord Brougham & Vaux 20 July 1835 at the Amphitheatre Liverpool' (Rose, R.E. Smith, Liverpool, 1836)

·TO THE PUBLIC.

I cannot let the fourth edition of my pamphlet go to press without warmly thanking my friends and the public at large for the very kind and liberal encouragement which I have received from them. The doubts which I felt in complying with the urgent request of my intimate friends and countrymen are now dispersed, and my anxieties have been amply repaid, for the unprecedented sale of my speech has exceeded my most sanguine expectations, and nothing now is left on my mind but the most heartfelt gratitude to all and each of my subscribers, collectively and individually.   R. Rose.

OPINIONS OF THE PRESS.

We have perused the Speech of Mr. Robert Rose, at the Brougham dinner, and must express our regret in not being able to extract a portion of it, as we are sure it cannot fail of being read with great interest by all who admire the beauties of the English language. The feeling which pervades it throughout is highly creditable to him.—*Liverpool Chronicle, September* 12.

We perceive that a committee of West Indians have published, in a neat form and at a cheap rate, a full and correct report of the able Speech delivered by their talented countryman, Mr. Rose, at the Brougham dinner, at the Amphitheatre. We received it too late to notice it more particularly now.—*Liverpool Journal, September* 12.

Mr. Rose's Speech.—We perceive that the speech of Mr. R. Rose, the young West Indian, which created such an impression at the dinner given to Lord Brougham, in the Amphitheatre, by the friends and members of the Mechanics' Institution, some time ago, has been printed in a separate form. The sentiments which Mr. Rose expresses in behalf of his persecuted brethren, and in reprobation of those accursed crimes, slavery and the slave trade, do honour alike to his head and heart.—*Mercury, September* 18.

Speech of Mr. Robert Rose, at the Brougham dinner, Liverpool.— The subjoined note is appended to Mr. Rose's Speech, and explains the irreverent and unseemly interruptions which he had to contend against :—" The members of a committee of West Indians, selected for the publication,"* &c. &c. So florid a speaker will be of immense advantage to the cause of " Civil and Religious Liberty."—*Liverpool Standard, September* 18.

* Vide page 15.

Mr. Rose's Speech.—We perceive that this pamphlet has already gone through a second edition. It fully merits an attentive perusal.—*Liverpool Journal, September* 19.

The Speech delivered by Mr. Rose, a gentleman of colour, at the dinner given to Lord Brougham, at the Amphitheatre, and which was so favourably received, has been printed in a separate form; and such has been the demand for it, that it has already reached a second edition.—*Times*

A SPEECH, &c.

JAMES AIKEN, Esq., having been called to the chair, on the departure of James Brancker, Esq., remarked that as the evening was so far advanced, several toasts on the list could not be given; but that there was one which, from its interest, he observed, ought not to be omitted, especially as he was happy to state that there was a gentleman present who could effectually reply to it, being a native of those islands which had so lately experienced its benefit, and one who, some years ago, might have been looked upon with disrespect, in consequence of former prejudices, yet owing, as he felt proud to say, to the very considerable progress that society had made in improvement, he had no doubt that in now introducing him to the company he would be looked upon in the same light, and listened to with the same kindness and attention, as those who had preceded him. He therefore wished the toast—" Civil and religious liberty all over the world," to take precedence of every thing else, and in proposing it called upon Mr. Rose* to answer to it.

* After Lord Brougham and many of the company had retired, there was a very interesting speech delivered by Mr. Rose, a gentleman of colour, several of whose poetical pieces have recently appeared in some of the Liverpool papers. We regret that Mr. Rose's speech was not earlier delivered, as we are convinced that it would have gratified his Lordship. The occasional interruptions which the speaker experienced proceeded from a very few gentlemen, who were probably of the number of those who, in that same Amphitheatre, vehemently applauded Mr. Borthwick, when he publicly lectured in justification of the colonial system.—We recommend the perusal of Mr. Rose's speech to those who, like ourselves, had retired from the meeting before it was delivered.—*Liverpool Mercury, July* 24.

4

Mr. Rose, a gentleman of colour, then spoke to the following effect:—

Mr. Chairman, Ladies, and Gentlemen,

I have too much respect for you to trespass long on your attention; and I can assure you that I would not thus have presumed to address you, were I not well aware that among so many liberal-minded men my feelings will be sympathized with, when you perceive that I am one in close connexion, or, more properly, in strong affinity, with the thousands, ay, myriads of the human race, who, I am proud to say, have ever experienced your kind consideration. In, therefore, trusting to the enthusiasm, to the importance of the occasion, I shall endeavour to fortify my mind so as entirely to overcome all feelings of diffidence, all conviction of incapability, and all those varied emotions which so frequently, yet naturally, arise to obstruct the inexperienced youth in the performance of what he knows to be an imperative duty; and which I, in relying on your indulgence, should indeed blame myself for neglecting, as such opportunities as the present may happen but once in the life of man.—(Cheers.)

Whilst joining enthusiastically in the exultant shouts with which we have hailed the presence of the intellectual Colossus of the age,—(cheers,)—I looked round me, and I could not refrain from asking myself, "Where are *my* countrymen?" Alas! they have been groaning under a bondage

5

similar to that in olden time inflicted by the task-masters of Egypt; and of them I *alone* am here, a free-born man, to express for them their deep obligations to him and to you. This pleasing task hath devolved on me *alone*; and this is, indeed, the proudest hour of my life, when I am so especially favoured above them as to have it in my power personally to thank their benefactors, among the foremost and most generous of whom how happy am I to recognise HENRY LORD BROUGHAM.—(Cheers.) In calling your attention to this subject, Gentlemen, I do it not with respect to its political sense; that is by no means my intention.—(Cries of "We know.") I pass over all forms and modes of forms, and all shades of partial and impartial opinion, to hasten at once to grasp the grand point and climax of my discourse, against which, I ween, there can be no candid or substantial objection raised, as universality is its basis, and in it is engendered and embodied every thing that is beauteous or holy in religion,—that is noble or pure in morality,—*charity and good will to all men;* and lean this individual's ideas one way, or that individual's another; be the reasoning faculties ever so much debased, enervated, or prostituted; let all the sophisms which have ever been adduced, be started against it in a mighty concatenation of encyclopædia array; still this grand principle, on which no eloquence can fully enough expatiate, stands, in its condensed strength,

6

as on a rock of ages, which is too firmly fixed to be cast asunder, or in the least particle shaken, by the conflicting discords of mankind: it flows from the everlasting fountain of justice and mercy; rising superior to all lowly distinctions, it directly appeals to the Godhead, and thence to the natural and ever durable laws between *man* and *man;* and by it, through it, and for it, every thing in this sublunary sphere lives, moves, and hath its being: it is to be found most active in this gem of the earth, this queen of the ocean; for

> " 'Tis Liberty that crowns Britannia's isle,
> And makes her barren rocks and her bleak mountains smile."
> (Great applause.)

I now, in reference to this, wish to draw your thoughts to the *degraded* state in which my countrymen have been held, (having been hitherto debarred all the advantageous effects of education and rational liberty,) as a means of comparing it to their present happier condition, and all the benefits which they now enjoy, particularly as they can now congratulate themselves that *slavery,* which once sounded so terrible and startling to every humane and well-disposed mind, is now but a name;— (cheers)—and that through your interposition, having stretched forth the protecting arm, *those* injured children of God,—*those* sufferers who have toiled and toiled through years of pain and misery, —*those* whose bread of affliction hath been steeped, alas! in the bitter cup of sorrow,—*those* who have

7

far too long been compelled to drink the turbid waters of cool mockery, and whose fate it hath been to be tormented by the scorpion stings of unfeeling and ruffian scorn,—are now elevated in the scale of social being! They have long laboured by the sweat of their brow—for *what* compensation?— *blows, stripes,* and the ignominious burdens imposed on them by self-made traffickers in human flesh, although their Christianity and boasted knowledge inform them that the almighty and omnific Ruler, who cares for the smallest insect in his extended works, has made of one blood all nations of the earth.—

> " He sees with equal eye, as God of all,
> A hero perish, or a sparrow fall."

But this beneficent order of Divine Providence hath been wickedly defeated by demons in human shape —(hear)—reckless of plaintive cries ascending to the supernal realms of Justice, and hastening on the oppressor's head the sure vengeance of Him *" who rides on the whirlwind and directs the storm."* Have not my countrymen been treated worse than *felons,* or *dogs,* or *reptiles* crawling upon the face of the earth?—(Hear, hear.)   Have they not been galled, jaded,—nay, torn from the bosom of their families,—torn from all their souls held dear, *never,* oh! *never* again to view the well-known fields where, like yourselves, they erewhile sported in all the innocence of boyhood,—doomed to drag out, in strict companionship with melancholy, oft-

times approaching to despair, their severe pittance
of existence, until death itself, whose aspect is
so grim and horrible to others, hath been hailed
by them with rapture : *but, thank God, their
chains have been struck from them !*—(Tremen-
dous cheering.) Their protectors have claimed
that rank for them, which, howsoever extorted
the reluctant confession may be, all must allow
they deserve. They are endowed with the same
rights, and gifted with the same privileges in
the creation, in common with all whom "nature,
the general parent," hath designated with the
marks of man.—(Loud cheers.) Even as some
time-honoured edifice, glittering with the mellow
radiance of vernal splendour, so hath the munifi-
cence of your benevolence imparted hallowed bril-
liance to a land where gloom was hovering, which
seemed almost bereft of hope and consigned to
wretchedness,—adding, as with a wand of magic,
new features to the scene, inasmuch as that land,
originally in appearance so like a garden of Eden,
which should never have been trampled on by the
oppressor, is now re-peopled with new forms, as it
were, with cheerful tones and merry countenances;
and I think—nay, I am sure—that they will *never,
never* prove themselves unworthy of your kindness.
(Cheers.) They breathe in free air,—they walk
erect,—they feel,—they reason,—(laughter)—they
can reason,—(laughter)—they move with limbs un-
shackled and with brow undaunted,—they sustain the

sacred dignity of humanity,—they exult in the glad consciousness of Liberty! and, as they can now do—what the animals or wild beasts of the woods could always do—(laughter)—roam at large over the ground: as they pace it with buoyant steps, I have no doubt they can discover that the herbs of the fields, and the flowers of the garden, flourish for them as well as for others of the human species: —(laughter)—and show me the wretch who dares to say they display no signs of intellect, and ought not to experience the advantages of knowledge.— (Interruption.)   Who is he, and where is he, who dares to hazard such an abominable assertion? Let him stand forward! I am here to answer him. —(Cries of " Personal.")   Gracious Heavens! is he so wedded to his lamentable dulness, or is he so immersed in his own filthy selfishness,—(cries of " Personal")—as to be dead to all human sympathy?   Do but point him out to me.—(Cries of " Stop," and partial hissing.)   Some of you may hiss, like serpents, but you do not possess the serpent's sting.—(Laughter.)   I have not been personal intentionally, but " the guilty flee when no man pursues."—(Loud laughter.)

[Here the Chairman interfered, beseeching them to give Mr. Rose a fair hearing.]

Mr. Rose.—It may be considered that I have gone too far;—(A cry of " Yes," and loud cries of " No," from all parts of the house)—but recollect, Gentlemen, that it has been owing to an over-

10

whelming sense of the intense and all-absorbing interest of the subject; recollect, that I cannot but feel, and feel deeply, the wrongs that have been heaped upon my countrymen,—those countrymen who, I am certain, never will cease to offer up their fervent supplications at the throne of Grace, for the benefactors of the rising generation, in the ardent hope that all the world will imitate the transcendent example which England sets, in the dissemination of the inestimable blessings of education.—(Cheers.) The *march of intellect* is greater than the *march of armies,* and England has with rapid strides out-stripped other countries in the race of glory; and how can she fail when she can boast of such master-spirits as a Henry Brougham, the bulwark of a nation's host; and when we glance at Liverpool, we survey with gratitude the public conduct of such personages as our late worthy Chairman, James Brancker, Esq., and his successor, James Aiken, Esq., who have ever been observed the first in their ranks for promoting every grade of im-provement with enterprise and spirit.—(Applause.)

Gentlemen,—I am afraid I have been trespass-ing too long on your patience.—(Loud cries of " No; go on.") I would not have taken up so much of your time had I not hoped I was not at all deviating from those wishes which are at your hearts, as well as at mine.—(" No, no.") I feel thankful for the reception I now meet with, and I shall tell my countrymen, when I return to them, how kindly I have been treated by you; and when for that purpose I commit myself to the waves of the boundless ocean, I shall soon tell them that they are but a mighty resemblance to that vast flood of knowledge which is now rushing onward, despite of every impediment. Above all, I shall tell my countrymen that I have thanked their advocates and defenders; and then, what being is there who will not envy my situation, when, surrounded by them, and by fresh tokens of improvement, I behold the smile of satisfaction beaming from their countenances, and, what is more, the quiet tears of heart-felt gratitude stealing down their cheeks, and hear their simultaneous prayer ascending to Heaven, that all nations, kindred, tongues, and people may henceforth be united in the circumambient bonds of sympathy, and raise the universal song of thanksgiving to the watchful Father of all.—(Applause.)

Gentlemen,—This is the first time of my ever appearing in public,—(hear, hear,)—and of having had the honour of addressing such a numerous and respectable audience: judge what my feelings must be. I should now conclude, but would fain say a few words on the *distinguished* personage we have seen this evening.—(Loud cheers.) I knew it would be grateful to all our thoughts, and cannot but give vent to the ebullitions of my excitement in such an auspicious hour as the present, for I am glad to find so many gentlemen of different creeds, denominations, and principles, have combined to

12

swell this large assembly, and have drowned all party animosities and prejudices, warmed with the strong desire of showing their personal regard to our eminent visitor. The respect which we have paid him is too frequently deferred till a great man's death! The amaranthine flowers of the past too often bloom over charnel-houses and the grave! When we contemplate the past meteors of the world, the smile of honest exultation is dashed with the tears of sorrow, and, as one of our first poets beautifully describes,—

> " Who hath not shared that calm, so still and deep,
> The voiceless thought which would not speak, but weep ;
> A holy concord, and a bright regret ;
> A glorious sympathy with suns that set ?"

But in turning to the living, what heart doth not bound with inward pleasure—what heart doth not feel ennobled with the idea that it can identify itself as palpitating to him who exists in the same age as Henry Lord Brougham?—(Enthusiastic cheers.) At some future day, when the Goddess of Knowledge, from her lofty temple, sounds the loud trump of Fame over his grave, what will it avail the dignified inhabitant who sleeps below, if that fame hath not been awarded to him in his life-time ? It is while he is living that that rank should be given to him which he so well deserves,—that rank which is already asserted for him by the *enlightened* of every nation !—(Loud cheers.)

When the whirlwind is hushed,—when a deep

knell is sounding, solemnly proclaiming that those contending emotions have subsided, which, in distracting the minds of men, might at moments alienate their good wishes from him who hath sacrificed all quiet enjoyments,—(cheers,)—and devoted his life to the public service!—(loud cheers)—when the tones which we have just heard are mute, those tones which have astonished us, as the emanations of the vivid intellectual energy of your first orator and statesman,—when pilgrims from the remotest corners of India, and from the most distant lands, come to venerate his tomb and do homage to his ashes, think, oh! think how *they* will envy *us* the enjoyment of *this* night!—(Cheers.) Then will tardy men perceive, when it is too late, what they have lost, and perceive but to mourn! A light will have been extinguished, an equal to which who can say will ever be replaced?—(Hear.) Then, granting even that there may have been some specks discernible in the orb of glory,—some slight taints blended with the rainbow and etherial colouring,—some little frailty incident to human nature, which would entirely have escaped notice in the shades which envelop the general mass, who move in comparative obscurity,—will it not still be mortifying to mark that he who hath towered above others, and stood unbowed to the tempest's shock, should have been so disproportionably, so wilfully misrepresented, by the minions of envy, who are ever on the watch, as if they, forsooth, were the never-failing concomitants of greatness, who, in order to bring the high more to the level of the low,—

> " Distort the truth, accumulate the lie,
>   And pile the Pyramid of calumny !"

But is this to be the *reward* of toil and talent? No! THE VIRTUOUS AND THE CANDID HEED THEM NOT,—they list not to their pestiferous and transitory breath; but sadly pause in their career to wonder how Lord Brougham could ever have had such enemies.—(Cries of " Too long for this late hour.")

Mr. ROSE.—Have patience; I am not now talking of *my* countrymen; I am talking of *yours*. It is now *your* turn.—(Laughter.)

When his slanderers,—(hear, hear,)—like the empty and ephemeral pageants of an hour, shall have vanished, without leaving a single record of usefulness behind them,—they who are but " dust in the balance, and found wanting,"—who cannot appreciate his worth, or appreciating it *secretly*, do him injustice *openly*,—when the swift stream of Time, with irresistible impulse, shall have swept away the very wrecks of those who, instead of being so clamorous against what they must ever despair of imitating, should rather go and "hide their diminished heads"—those Lilliputians who have dared to assail the invulnerable GIANT!—(tremendous cheering)—only expose their impotency, for ere long they must all powerlessly shrink into their caverns, and amid the inevitable wreck of years will be crumbled into

15

atoms;—when they, with their vile slanders,—(hear) which have passed by him heedlessly, "as the idle wind which he respects not," shall be buried in the wide and unfathomable gulph of Cimmerian darkness, together with all the despicable tribe of puny creatures who have dared to echo in utterance to them,—then, oh think how triumphantly will the Spirit of the memory of Henry Lord Brougham, the Champion of Knowledge and Freedom, start from the night of future ages, *spurning* at oblivion,

> " Like some tall cliff that lifts its awful form,
> Swells from the vale and midway leaves the storm;
> Tho' round its breast the rolling clouds are spread,
> *Eternal sunshine* settles on its head !"

(This speech was delivered with much warmth and animation, particularly the latter passage, which drew down the most enthusiastic applause.)

The members of a committee of West Indians, selected for the publication of the foregoing Speech, think it their duty to remark, that a full report of it is rather injured, from the interruptions which Mr. Rose experienced; and it is their wish, in publishing this, to do him justice, as far as possible, under existing circumstances, in the eyes of the public and of his countrymen, to whom copies of it will be transmitted. The annoyance which he received, and which they exceedingly regret should have occurred, proceeded from a *very few Americans*, who were the only persons who appeared to evince no sympathy with the object which he had in view. This they consider due to him to state, as many casual observers might be disposed to infer that he trespassed too long on the attention of the meeting. When attending on him to communicate their project, he kindly offered to correct the report, and likewise expressed a desire that the proceeds arising from its sale should be appropriated to charitable purposes.

Speech of Mr. Robert Rose, at the Brougham Dinner, Liverpool.— When Buonaparte found the extreme difficulty of conciliating the British people, he struck out a new path, and promising the co-operation of France for the grand object of the abolition of slavery, half succeeded in winning a powerful party to his cause. Could a higher compliment be paid to any nation, than by evincing the effort to obtain its smiles in proffering aid to the cause of humanity! Holding fast the aphorism of doing as we would be done by, we have ever been the warmest advocate of liberty, both for the black and for the white. It is, therefore, with a feeling of deep interest that we refer our readers to the intelligent speech of Mr. Rose—liberal, as well as intelligent—for, with the exception of a just eulogium on Lord Brougham and the friends of freedom, it exhibits no political allusions, and pertinently notices that " the *march of intellect* is greater than *the march of armies*."—*Liverpool Weekly Magazine, Sept.* 26.

Shortly will be Published,

ILLUSIONS OF THE PAST,

From the *Manuscripts* of R. ROSE, a West Indian; dedicated (by permission) to the Right Hon. Henry Lord Brougham.

Longman and Co., London; J. Walmsley and Co., Church-street, Liverpool.

THOUGHTS ON PHILOSOPHY,

AND

ESSAYS ON ENGLISH ORATORY,

BY R. ROSE,

Will be Published afterwards.

E. SMITH AND CO., PRINTERS, LORD-STREET, LIVERPOOL.

Bibliography

Manchester Notes and Queries, Vol. Vi June 1885

Alston, D., *Slaves and Highlanders,* Edinburgh UP, 2021

Bickford, James, *Autobiography of Christian Labour in the West Indies, Demerara, Victoria, New South Wales, and South Australia 1838–1888,* London, 1890

Edwards, P. and Dabydeen, D., *Black Writers in Britain 1760–1890,* Edinburgh UP, 1991

Fischer, S.R., *The History of Writing,* BCA, 2005

Froude, J.A., *The English in the West Indies,* Longmans, Green & Co., 1888

Lean, J.H., 'The Secret Lives of Slaves in Berbice 1819–1827', PhD Thesis, University of Canterbury, 2002

Olusoga, D., 'The Ties that bind us…' in 'Cotton Capital: a special investigation', *The Guardian,* April 2023

Rogerson, J.B. (ed.), *The Festive Wreath,* Bradshaw and Blacklock, 1832

Salmon, C.S., *The Caribbean Confederation,* Cassell & Company Ltd, 1888

Singh, I. and Mahoney, M., *Indian Indentureship 1834–1917,* UK National Archives Outreach Team, 2020

Thompson, A.O., *Unprofitable Servants: Crown Slaves in Berbice, Guiana, 1803-1831,* University of West Indies Press, 2002

West, Shearer, 'Black Victorians: Black people in British Art 1800–1900', *Victorian Literature and Culture,* Vol. 35, No. 1, 2007, pp.329–34

Woodman, D., *The Story of Manchester,* The History Press, 2017

Websites

https://www.britishempire.co.uk
https://www.britishnewspaperarchive.co.uk
www.jstor.org/stable/40347138
www.ucl.ac.uk/lbs/
www.vc.id.au/tb/bgcolonistsR.html

Index

Dear Reader,

We hope you have enjoyed this book, but why not share your views on social media? You can also follow our pages to see more about our other products: facebook.com/penandswordbooks or follow us on X @penswordbooks

You can also view our products at www.pen-and-sword.co.uk (UK and ROW) or www.penandswordbooks.com (North America).

To keep up to date with our latest releases and online catalogues, please sign up to our newsletter at: www.pen-and-sword.co.uk/newsletter

If you would like a printed catalogue with our latest books, then please email: enquiries@pen-and-sword.co.uk or telephone: 01226 734555 (UK and ROW) or email: uspen-and-sword@casematepublishers.com or telephone: (610) 853-9131 (North America).

We respect your privacy and we will only use personal information to send you information about our products.

Thank you!